The CV Book

Your definitive guide to writing the perfect CV

James *nnes*

Prentice Hall
is an imprint of

PEARSON

Harlow, England • London • New York • Boston • San Francisco • Toronto • Sydney • Singapore • Hong Kong
Tokyo • Seoul • Taipei • New Delhi • Cape Town • Madrid • Mexico City • Amsterdam • Munich • Paris • Milan

PEARSON EDUCATION LIMITED

Edinburgh Gate
Harlow CM20 2JE
Tel: +44 (0)1279 623623
Fax: +44 (0)1279 431059
Website: www.pearsoned.co.uk

First published in Great Britain in 2009

© James Innes 2009

The right of James Innes to be identified as author of this work has been asserted by him in accordance with the Copyright, Designs and Patents Act 1988.

ISBN: 978-0-273-72174-1

British Library Cataloguing-in-Publication Data
A catalogue record for this book is available from the British Library

Library of Congress Cataloging-in-Publication Data
Innes, James, 1975-
  The CV book : your definitive guide to writing the perfect CV / James Innes.
    p. cm
  ISBN 978-0-273-72174-1 (pbk.)
  1. Résumés (Employment) 2. Cover letters. I. Title.
  HF5383.I55 2009
  650.14'2--dc22
                    2009020973

10 9 8 7 6 5 4 3 2 1
13 12 11 10 09

Typeset in 9.5/13pt in Din Regular by 30
Printed in Great Britain by Henry Ling Ltd., at the Dorset Press, Dorchester, Dorset

The publisher's policy is to use paper manufactured from sustainable forests.

The CV Book

....

This book is dedicated to my parents.
To my mother, Elisabeth – for teaching me everything that was ever of
any real importance.
To my father, Don – for guiding me and protecting me while always giving me
the freedom to go my own way and find my own path in life.

....

Contents

Acknowledgements

I would like to thank all of my colleagues and clients at The CV Centre, both present and past. Without them it would clearly not have been possible for me to write *The CV Book*. In particular, I would like to thank Susan Staley, who has closely supported me in the production of this book. I would also like to thank Katy Wilson, Amanda Jackson, Sharon Williamson, Sean McAlister and Margaret Hall.

I would additionally like to thank Richard Day at Beaufort Web Design for his significant contribution to the online elements of this book.

Special thanks also go to the team at Pearson, in particular Samantha Jackson, Caroline Jordan and Laura Blake. I couldn't have had better publishers behind me. Assistance in checking and correcting the text was also provided by Don Elkins, Elisabeth Elkins and Malcolm Innes.

Finally, I would like to thank Delphine Vaucanson for her love and support and her toleration of my frequently working very excessively long hours!

Introduction

Dear Reader

'Why do some people almost always get the job they want?'

Because *their* CV wins them an interview – and 99 per cent *don't*!

As a professional CV writer, I see every single day which CVs really achieve results. This puts me in a unique position, enabling me to bring you the very best of what I have learned – and helping you to create a truly exceptional CV.

What exactly is a 'curriculum vitae'?

'Curriculum vitae' is a Latin term and translates as 'the course of one's life'. The simplest dictionary definition says that a curriculum vitae is 'a summary of your academic and work history'. Well, that's basically true, but I see a curriculum vitae (commonly abbreviated, of course, to CV) as more of a personal sales brochure, one which should be very carefully written and presented to ensure that you have the best possible chance of getting the job you want – to really showcase your talent.

It is not an autobiography. Simply writing down a list of everything you have done and everything you know will not guarantee you an interview – in fact it will just bore the socks off the recruiter and undoubtedly count against you.

You should never lose sight of the fact that the primary aim of your CV is purely and simply to win you an interview.

What are the advantages of a properly presented and well-written CV?

It is vitally important to see matters from the recruiters' or prospective employers' perspective.

They're often faced with a pile of many hundreds of CVs to review – for just one vacancy. Almost a third of recruiters' admit to only reading a CV for a minute before deciding whether to interview the candidate. In fact, many admit to spending even less time! Twenty to 30 seconds is quite common.

They simply do not have the time to read them all in any depth. They're much more interested in getting out of the office and getting to the pub! In their initial sift, they will very likely be looking for reasons to discard your application, not for reasons to retain it. So how do you make your CV stand out? How do you maximise your chances of being among the ten or so candidates they decide to invite for interview?

My expertise in creating a truly professional CV is based on careful research into what recruiters really want from job applicants. This enables me to determine exactly what to put in, exactly what to leave out, and what kind of a 'spin' to put on a CV, to ensure that it will stand right out from the competition. Getting it right is the difference between getting your foot in the door for an interview, or ending up in the 'no thank you' pile – also known as the bin!

You need to help the recruiters as much as possible, since they see sifting through CVs as a chore and want it to be over as quickly as possible (remember, there's that pint waiting for them down the road!). They do not know you and they don't know what you're capable of – this is where you have to sell yourself.

What can this book do to help you?

You're reading this book for one reason – to find out what makes an exceptional CV. Clearly, you already realise just how important a document your CV is – in fact, it is probably the most important tool during your job hunt, so getting it right is absolutely essential. It is also one of the few aspects of your job hunt that you are really in control of.

CV writing can be a tricky subject – part art, part science – and there is no perfect solution that will suit everybody and every case. However, in *The CV Book* I aim to demonstrate exactly what you should and shouldn't do when writing your CV. No matter what your age, background, job or level of experience, I will help you to create a CV that really works for you.

This book condenses the same proven methodology I use every day with my clients and contains all the tips and – dare I say it – tricks, that you need. I will cut through all the debate and opinion about CVs and show you what really works from the recruiters' point of view – what I have *proved* to work.

The CV Centre website

I have made a commitment to readers of this book to provide numerous features to complement the book online at The CV Centre's website: **http://www.ineedacv.co.uk**. I also provide you with the opportunity to make contact with my team and I directly. Features include:

> ➤ The CV Centre Forum: you can exchange comments and ideas with other readers and also pose specific questions directly to members of The CV Centre team, including myself.
>
>   **http://www.ineedacv.co.uk/forum**
>
> ➤ The CV Centre Blog: a regular column, drawing on specific questions, topics and problems raised in the forum and elaborating on them in detail.
>
>   **http://www.ineedacv.co.uk/blog**
>
> ➤ The CV Centre Tools: free CV review, job vacancy database, templates download, etc.

As a reader of *The CV Book,* access to all these tools and facilities is free. Throughout the book you will be given special links taking you directly to the pages in question.

Special offer

I have also prepared a special offer for you. If, after reading this book, you decide you would like one of our team to help further develop and perfect your CV, when you place an order with us we will throw in our CV distribution service entirely for free.

With our extensive database of contacts, we can distribute your CV by email to a wide range of quality recruitment agencies and employers matching your requirements. Quite simply, the more people who see your CV, the better your chances of finding the job you want.

Simply visit the following page on our site to take advantage of this exclusive offer.

http://www.ineedacv.co.uk/9780273721741

Thank you for choosing *The CV Book*. I have set out to write the most complete and up-to-date guide to CV writing on the market today – a definitive guide to CV writing. I trust that you will both enjoy it and find it useful. And I look forward to meeting you on our forum should you have any further questions.

I really want to help you get the job – and the future – that you want.

James Innes

Kind regards
James Innes
Managing Director
The CV Centre

How to use this book

There's no doubt about it; this book covers a lot of ground.

However, I appreciate that you may well need to send your CV off later today and simply might not have the time to read everything. I have therefore provided a 'fast track' below by listing the top 15 questions that people ask when writing a CV. This should help you to quickly and easily answer the vast majority of the points that are troubling you.

Once you've found the answers to your questions, before finishing off your CV, do make sure you spare five minutes to read Part 9, My five top tips. If you only had time to read one page of *The CV Book*, this is the page I would most like you to have read. It encapsulates the most important principles that I cover in the book. Make an effort to accommodate all these when writing your CV and you'll immediately be well above average.

Writing a CV can be a lonely task. But you're not alone. There's someone I'd like to introduce you to ...

CASE STUDY | *Meet Jane Bloggs*

Throughout this book, I will be using a case study to better illustrate the ideas and principles in question and to help bring them to life. This will also help you to better understand the issues raised and make it easier for you to apply the concepts to your own CV.

Everyone is different, of course, and there is no one individual to whom all ideas will apply, but I have settled on an example which the majority of readers will be able to readily identify with.

Meet Jane Bloggs!

I won't tell you too much about her because we'll get to know her a lot better in the chapters to come. But, for now, I can tell you that Jane is 30 years old and works as a Sales Manager for a large stationery retailer, following previous experience in the food and drink sector. Having completed her BA (Hons) in Marketing and Advertising, she's keen to return to the food and drink sector and branch out into a combined sales and marketing role. She's also hoping that her next move will increase her level of responsibility and autonomy and, perhaps more importantly, increase her pay packet!

The Top 15 questions that people ask when writing a CV

Right, if you're short on time and need answers fast then this section is for you.

The chances are you've got at least one – if not more – of the following questions on your mind.

I have compiled this list based on the questions we most frequently get asked at The CV Centre. It contains the top 15 most common questions concerned job hunters ask about CV writing – the questions that come up regularly every single day. If you're reading this book, then it's more than likely that you will be asking yourself many of the same questions.

Each question is listed alongside details as to where in this book you can find the answers you are looking for.

All the answers to these questions and many more can be found within *The CV Book*. And if you have a question to which you can't find the answer then why not visit our online forum:

http://www.ineedacv.co.uk/forum

The top 15 questions

1 Which font do you recommend?

Chapter 1 Aesthetics and presentation: looking good on paper

2 Should I use bullet points or full paragraphs?

Chapter 2 Content and style: what to say and how to say it

3 Which type of CV should I use?

Chapter 3 Structure: which type of CV is right for you?

4 How long should my CV be?

Chapter 3 Structure: which type of CV is right for you?

5 What contact details should I put on my CV – and where?

Chapter 4 Personal details

6 Should I put my date of birth on my CV?

Chapter 4 Personal details

7 Should I include a personal profile and/or objective?

Chapter 5 Professional profile

Chapter 6 Objective

8 Do I need to list absolutely all my exam grades?

Chapter 7 Education and qualifications

9 Do I mention every job I've had or just my most recent one?

Chapter 8 Career history

10 Should I include a *Key Skills* section?

Chapter 9 Key skills

11 What's the consensus on whether or not to include an *Achievements* section?

Chapter 10 Achievements

12 What sort of thing is it best to put under *Interests and Activities*?

Chapter 12 Interests and activities

13 Should I include a photo?

Part 3 The 15 most common CV writing mistakes – and how to avoid them!

14 What should I do about gaps in my employment history?

Chapter 13 Ten solutions for ten potential problems

15 Is it a good idea to tailor my CV for each specific vacancy?

Part 5 Tailoring your CV

PART 1

LAYING THE FOUNDATIONS: GETTING THE BASICS RIGHT

Chapter **1**

Aesthetics and presentation: looking good on paper

Presentation, presentation, presentation. The very first step you should take in creating your CV is to stop to think for a moment about how you are going to present it. Most jobseekers don't realise that the way their CV is presented can often be of more value in getting to the next stage of the application process than the information itself. You will make an impression on the reader even before they read a single word. Presentation can make all the difference between success and failure.

If the presentation of the CV is thoroughly professional then the applicant immediately gives the impression of being thoroughly professional themself. But the opposite also applies: a poorly presented CV will give a poor impression of you. Never forget that you are marketing yourself – and the way you present your CV can have an impact on the reader that is almost as powerful as the actual content.

However, it is rare for me to come across a CV which couldn't stand some improvement to its presentation and layout. There's normally always at least one area that can be 'tweaked' to improve the visual impact of the CV – and often half a dozen!

Why is presentation so important?

Surveys show that badly presented and poorly written CVs are much more of a turn-off to recruiters than more obvious gaffs, such as showing up late for interview or even swearing in an interview.

It's logical really – faced with hundreds of CVs it's all too easy to just chuck a poor CV straight in the bin and that's the end of the story. However, when someone turns up for an interview, even if they don't make a great first impression, at least they've got their foot in the door. That's a significant advantage – and yet another reason why getting your CV right is so important.

Good presentation can attract the recruiter to read through your CV instead of someone else's and will instantly give them a positive feeling about you. However, poor presentation will hide any information you want the recruiter to see and will build a negative impression of you before you have even had a chance to progress to the interview stage. Your CV will simply end up in the bin (or possibly as a paper dart!).

You may have spent many years obtaining skills and qualifications but, if they are not presented correctly, you won't achieve your career potential. This would be a terrible – and unnecessary – waste. But it's all too common.

Enhancing the presentation of a CV is very much the cosmetic surgery of the CV writing world. Content is clearly more important – and we'll go into this in more detail in the next chapter – but aesthetics are also critical in making the right impact on the reader. First impressions are absolutely vital – and up to a quarter of CVs are immediately binned by recruiters because of poor presentation.

The key areas to address

To help you present yourself to the best of your ability I'm going to discuss in detail a number of key areas.

May I first of all say that I readily expect you will possibly be making the majority of your applications by email rather than by post – and any talk of paper choice or envelopes in this chapter is clearly going to be irrelevant when it comes to submitting your application electronically.

However, at least for the time being, there are just as many (if not more) vacancies where you are still expected to apply by good old-fashioned snail mail.

We will, in any case, be talking more about emailing your application in Part 6, Digital considerations.

For now, let's assume you'll be sending it by post.

Choosing your paper

Your first decision will probably be what type of paper to use.

Make sure you use good quality A4 (no other size) paper that is not flimsy but not too thick either. 100gsm is ideal (80gsm is acceptable). White is fine. But slightly off-white (e.g. what is known as 'high white' – a very subtle cream effect) may be even better – because it adds a 'touch of class' that plain white paper lacks and it also sets your CV apart, because the majority of people still use plain white (also known as 'brilliant white').

You most certainly shouldn't use coloured or patterned paper.

BLOOPER!

There's the classic story of the candidate who (perhaps wanting to demonstrate that he had a sense of humour?) submitted a CV on 'Garfield the Cat' paper! If you're applying to work in a cat sanctuary and your prospective boss is a huge fan of Garfield, then this might possibly give you an advantage. But in the other 99.9999 per cent of cases it certainly won't!

Typeface and font

It should go without saying that your CV should be word-processed, not typewritten or, perish the thought, handwritten. Yet I still do occasionally see handwritten or typewritten CVs from time to time. Perhaps even worse is a CV which has been originally word-processed but which has then had details added or corrected by hand. I can say with almost total certainty that a CV like this would never win an interview, yet more than once have I seen such CVs.

Anyway, assuming that you will indeed be word-processing your CV, here's a couple of quick definitions for you – because the key terms typeface and font are frequently conflated:

Typeface: a style of printed script, e.g. Times New Roman, Arial or Verdana.

Font: a subdivision of a typeface, e.g. bold or italic, including a denotation of size – traditionally measured in 'points'.

[NB: these definitions are somewhat simplified but are more than sufficient for our purposes.]

Typeface

I would strongly recommend that you remain conservative with your choice of typeface.

Presentation is, of course, a personal issue and some people will prefer certain typefaces to others – for example, teachers tend to like Comic Sans. However, it is important to realise that the easiest to read typefaces will get you the positive presentation points! We generally use mainstream typefaces such as Times New Roman and Arial, as they are professional, easy to read and get results.

Avoid unusual typefaces, since they are generally harder to read, not only for humans but for automated scanning software. It is critical not to go over the top with fancy layouts, typefaces, etc. They can detract and confuse. A clear, conservative impression is always preferable, except in specific cases such as architecture, graphic design, etc., where you are entitled to demonstrate a little more creative licence. But, in general, don't stray too far from the standards such as Times New Roman or Arial.

Font

Bold: it's certainly a good idea to make use of bold type but it should be used sparingly – to highlight headings and separate sections. It can also be used to draw the reader's eye towards key information – for example degree titles. But avoid using it to highlight less important information, for example employers' names.

Italic: if you want to highlight particular sections of text then you should generally use bold, not italic. Italic, however, can – and should – be used if you need to quote the names of publications, i.e. books, newspapers, magazines, journals, etc. I also favour using it for your *Professional Profile* and *Objective* (more about those later...).

Size: try to keep to 11 or 12 point in general. You can make very limited use of 10 point and you can of course use 13 point or larger for main headings, including your name at the top of the CV. But the majority of the text should either be 11 or 12 point. And you should keep your headings consistent in size and the body copy consistent as well.

Break these rules at your peril. I have seen plenty of CVs where the writers have been so keen to cram everything in that they have resorted to 9 or 10 point throughout – and the result is very tiring indeed to read.

BLOOPER!

Some candidates are so desperate to fill up empty space that they use 14 point throughout – the result being that their CV ends up looking like a book for toddlers!

Colour

You should normally only use black ink. In certain cases it can be acceptable to make limited use of colour, but the general rule is to stick to black. I once saw a CV that used four different colours – and that is clearly excessive. Your reader is expecting a black-and-white document and, whilst it can sometimes be good to stand out from the crowd, using colour to do so is not a technique I would generally recommend.

You may own a high-quality colour laser printer with which to print your CV but, if you are emailing your CV to prospective recruiters, what sort of printers will they have? A CV containing colour may look very attractive on screen but can lose a lot of its appeal when printed on a poor-quality colour printer or, more likely, a standard office black-and-white printer. It is also often unsuitable for photocopying.

What is white space?

You need to carefully control your use of white space, presenting the information clearly and comprehensively – and with style – but within the limitations of the total space available.

'But, what is white space?' I hear you ask!

'White space' is a term often used by designers to designate those parts of a page which are 'left blank' (or, assuming you're using white paper, left white, i.e. not printed upon). Another commonly used and perhaps more meaningful term is 'empty space'. But I'm personally quite fond of the term 'breathing space' – because that describes what white space is intended for – to give the reader some breathing space. It's not simply blank space; it's at least half of the document you are designing and getting the right balance between white space and non-white (or 'positive') space is vital if you are to maximise readability.

The key to using white space effectively is to realise that its purpose is:

> To provide 'breathing space' for the readers, so that they are not overwhelmed with a solid block of hard-to-read text.
> To group together related content and separate disparate content.

TOP TIP

It's also important to allow space around a CV, particularly on a second page, for the reader to make notes. Not all recruiters will scribble all over your CV but I, and many others, certainly will.

Space is clearly at a premium when you are creating a CV. There's so much you could say and yet so little space to say it all in. But the answer isn't to strip out the white space. The answer is to be highly selective and concise in terms of the content you include – and we'll discuss that in greater detail in later chapters. A page with minimal white space generally comes across as cluttered and difficult to read – and this is definitely not going to help you get that job.

How to handle white space

White space includes your margins (top, bottom, left and right), linespacing, gaps between sections and tab spacing.

Spacing is – like all design issues – subjective, and a CV that might appear cramped to one person may appear too widely spaced to another. You should simply endeavour to strike a balance.

Margins: keep them wide. The top margin shouldn't drop below 1.5cm, nor should it exceed 3cm. 2cm/2.5cm is perfect. And the bottom margin should normally fall between 1cm and 2cm, although it is related to the top margin and should generally be 0.5cm/1cm smaller than the top margin – this is, as you will discover, visually important. Left and right margins should remain within the range of 1.5cm–2.5cm.

Header: the header should always start at least 1.25cm from the edge because not all printers can print closer than 1.25cm to the edge of a page.

Footer: the footer should also never start less than 1.25cm from the edge. As for what to place in it, the footer simply needs to say 'Page 1 of x' – even if your CV is only one page long. However, if you need to conjure up a little extra bit of room on a one-page CV then it is also perfectly acceptable to replace the 'Page 1 of 1' with 'References are available on request'. This is a useful trick to get that little extra bit of space where needed.

Line-spacing between text: you should always stick to standard single line-spacing, rather than, for example, double-spacing your CV.

Line-spacing between sections: the ideal for this is really 16 point. It is fine to use 14 point if space is short, but any less than this is to be avoided – far better to reduce the page margins or text size instead. And, of course, a little more than 16 point is acceptable if need be.

Justification: I recommend that the main text of your CV is 'fully justified'. This means that it is aligned to both the left and right margins with extra space automatically added between words as necessary (like this book). It creates a nice, clean look along both the left and right sides of the page. This is easy to achieve with word-processing software.

Beyond the first page: if your CV runs to more than one page then it's a good idea for the text on the second page (and subsequent pages, if applicable) to start lower than that on the first. Given that you will be stapling the pages together, if the text on the second page starts too high up it'll be difficult to read because the staple will get in the way.

Readability

Readability is defined as the ease with which a reader can absorb the meaning of your words. The more readable your writing is, the more effectively it will communicate to your reader. Research shows that working to ensure readability can have a positive impact on comprehension, retention and reading speed – and increases the chance that the reader will bother continuing to the end of the document.

We have already talked about the importance of selecting appropriate typefaces and controlling your use of white space – and all of this does contribute to a highly readable document.

But there's more to it than that.

You still have one further weapon up your sleeve ...

Bullet points

In case you're not sure what bullet points (also known as simply 'bullets') are, they're the small dots, squares, dashes, or arrows that can be used to introduce items in a list, for example:

> This is a bullet point.
> And so is this.

In today's fast-paced world, recruiters no longer have the time to read large, solid blocks of prose. They need to extract the information they need – and they need to do it fast. Long paragraphs of prose are tiresome for a recruiter to read right through and, as a result, many simply won't bother.

And this is where bullet pointing comes in, although, unfortunately, so many people fail to use it to their advantage within their CV. Whilst I wouldn't recommend you use bullet pointing everywhere – and I would actually recommend against it for your *Professional Profile* (See Chapter 5 'Professional profile') – I would very strongly recommend its use in your *Career History*.

Some people worry that using bullet points will take up more room on their CV than writing in solid prose. Whilst bullet points can potentially take up more room, if you word your CV carefully and concisely they shouldn't do so – and the positive impact on readability cannot be overstated.

How long should your bullet points be? Well, you should try to avoid bullet points that are only five or six words long. It's much better, visually, to aim for bullet points that at least fill the width of the page – or even 'spill' over onto a second line.

If you're faced with a stack of short bullet points then you should either rephrase them so as to increase the word count or you should amalgamate them with other bullet points so that you end up with fewer but longer bullet points.

TOP TIP

You should try to keep the length of your bullet-pointed lines more or less consistent. If they're all different lengths then it can look rather tatty.

Consistency of layout

A disorganised layout makes it hard for recruiters to extract the information they need.

Remember that most recruiters will be working under significant time pressure – and they won't waste their time trying to pick out the information they need from a poorly organised layout. You'll simply end up in the bin.

The formatting you use for your CV should be consistent from beginning to end. Any inconsistencies should be carefully eliminated.

So many CVs have errors in formatting, which means that some lines are indented more than others, some sections have more space between them than others, etc.

This just looks shoddy – and communicates a pretty poor impression to the reader. If you can't be bothered to take the time to perfect your CV, then why should they be wasting their time reading it?

As well as consistency within the CV itself, if you are enclosing a cover letter with your CV (which you normally will be), both documents should match in style, ensuring a fully coordinated image. As the saying goes: image is everything.

Graphics

Computer software – and the Internet – make it very easy to quickly generate graphics which you can then use in word-processed documents.

But just because it's easy to do so doesn't necessarily mean that you should do so.

Should you, for example, include the logos of the organisations you have worked for?

Personally, I would advise against it – they can all too easily distract attention from the all-important content.

Good presentation is intended to make a document's content easier to read, not to usurp it.

You can of course use appropriate graphical devices, such as plain horizontal lines, to help separate different sections of your CV – but don't overdo it. The correct use of graphics is to help structure your CV – not to decorate it.

Photos

People often include photos of themselves on their CV. Don't! Unless you are applying to be a model or wish to work as an actor/actress, then including a photo with/on your CV is definitely not recommended – at least not within the UK.

The whole point of a CV is that recruiters have a brief, factual description of your abilities, and photographs often allow them, rightly or wrongly, to develop a preconceived idea of you as a person – and this might well count against you. They may have an irrational aversion to facial hair for example! An interview is the most appropriate place for the recruiter to first see an applicant, not the CV.

Even if you do look like Brad Pitt or Kate Moss (and I don't think many of us do; personally I look nothing like Kate Moss ...) it isn't a good idea. People *will* discriminate – whether there are laws in place to ban them from doing so or not. This is a point which often confuses many of our foreign clients – because it is still perfectly normal in Europe and elsewhere to include a photo. But definitely not in the UK.

If you must include a photograph (and some recruiters/employers will insist on it, even though it comes very close to flouting anti-discrimination legislation) then make sure it is an appropriately professional passport-style photograph.

BLOOPER!

I've seen a wide range of interesting photos on CVs in my time, including one candidate who astonishingly included a photograph of herself wearing a bikini! (No, I didn't give her an interview.)

There are those who point out that 'a picture speaks a thousand words' and that the use of photography is vitally important in marketing.

Yes, photography is extremely important in marketing and advertising. Yes, your CV is a marketing document which advertises you to prospective employers. But the biggest hurdle you're up against is that it is not accepted practice in the UK to include a photograph and, whilst it's often great to stand out from the crowd, this is decidedly not a method that is recommended.

If you're sending your CV by email then the inclusion of a photo can also cause problems with anti-virus software. Your CV could be automatically deleted!

Printing

In an ideal world, you would print your CV using a high-quality laser printer. Print quality does make a difference. If you don't have access to a laser printer then you should obviously try to use the best printer you can get your hands on.

If your CV runs to more than one page always print it on separate sheets. Never print on both sides, even if it's high-quality paper and does-n't show through. The vast majority of people print on separate sheets rather than back-to-back so a recruiter won't be expecting print on both sides of the page – and may well overlook a large proportion of your CV as a result. I know it may seem wasteful and not very good for the environ-ment but you don't really have much choice I'm afraid.

One final word of warning is that you should never, ever photocopy your CV. Always use original prints.

Stapling

To staple or not to staple?

If your CV runs to more than one page, then it is generally recom-mended to attach the pages to each other by placing a single staple in the top left-hand corner. Don't just paperclip or, even worse, send loose sheets. If people are scanning CVs on receipt then it may be a slight nui-sance for them but not as bad as your two-page CV getting split in half.

Envelopes

When sending your CV (and cover letter) by post, I would definitely recommend choosing envelopes that match the paper your CV is printed on. A coordinated image can really impress. It is fair to say that in many cases recruiters won't open the envelope themselves (and that the envelope will subsequently go straight in the bin) but, particularly in smaller organisations, they often will.

As for size, some people recommend A4 (known as 'C4' when it comes to envelopes) because this means you won't have to fold your CV. Personally, I am against this, because a large A4 envelope with just two or three sheets of paper inside is a lot more likely to get crushed, crumpled or otherwise damaged in transit. And using a hard-backed envelope is definitely overkill.

I would simply recommend the C5 size of envelope – equivalent to a sheet of A4 folded in half. Folding your CV has obvious aesthetic drawbacks – and less obvious ones, for example it can make your CV harder to scan. However, on balance, I feel its advantages outweigh its disadvantages.

At a stretch, you could use the DL size of envelope – equivalent to an A4 sheet folded in three. But never use anything smaller than this.

BLOOPER!

I have seen too many applications folded in four or worse. It isn't an origami competition!

Exceptions to the rules

There aren't many exceptions to the rules I've laid out in this chapter but, if you work within a highly creative and artistic field, then you may be able to bend – or even break – some of the rules. But I'll cover this in Chapter 14 'Special cases – professions where the rules are different'.

Chapter **2**

Content and style: what to say and how to say it

It is of course extremely important to phrase your information in such a way as to sell yourself as effectively as possible.

Your CV is your personal sales brochure and needs to be copy-written accordingly.

It is also important to strike the right balance between too little and too much text. To achieve this, you're going to need to be very careful as to how you phrase yourself.

Person, pronouns and verbs

There's a lot of confusion as to the 'person' in which you should write your CV.

If you're not sure what a 'grammatical person' is then allow me to explain:

In English, we have three grammatical persons, each of which are denoted by different 'personal pronouns':

> ➤ 'I' (and 'we') denote the first person.

> ➤ 'You' denotes the second person (both singular and plural).

> ➤ 'He', 'she', 'it' (and 'they') denote the third person.

The verb which follows these personal pronouns will often take a different form dependent on the person involved (and whether it is singular or plural). One of the most extreme – and most common – examples is the verb 'to be':

> ➤ I am.

> ➤ You are.

> ➤ He is.

However, depending on the tense, most verbs vary in one way or another. I'll take the verb 'to possess' as an example:

> ➤ I possess.

> ➤ You possess.

> ➤ He possesses.

To make life even more complicated, these pronouns come in a variety of different forms. The ones I've mentioned above are 'nominative' (or 'subjective') pronouns – but there are also accusative (or 'objective'), genitive (or 'possessive') and even reflexive forms:

> ➤ For the first person these are me, my/mine and myself.

> ➤ For the third-person masculine they are him, his and himself.

> ➤ For the third-person feminine they are her, her/hers and herself.

Some schools of thought will say that your CV should be written in the first person; others will say it should be written in the third person. The problem is that the individuals behind these different schools of thought often don't really understand what they're talking about! The terms 'first person' and 'third person' are frequently misunderstood.

It is obvious that you will have to choose either the first person or the third person when writing your CV. It's one or the other – and my recommendation would be to use the third person, not the first person.

The words 'I' and 'me' are often used repeatedly in homemade CVs. Making a CV too personal by writing in the first person:

> can make it hard not to sound arrogant or egocentric

> tends to come across as rather unprofessional

> is simply too informal for the circumstances.

'I this …', 'I that …', 'I the other …', 'me, me, me!' This is not the impression you want to give the reader.

It might seem unnatural to write a document about yourself and yet never use either 'I' or 'me' but recruitment experts generally agree that this is the best way to do it. Don't give your reader I-strain!

The third person can sound a little stuffy at times, but it generally reads better and comes across as more professional. It gives you greater scope to brag about yourself without actually sounding as if you're bragging!

However, I'm certainly not saying you should litter your CV with 'he', 'she', 'his', 'her', etc. either.

The very best solution is not only to use the third person but to also keep your use of all pronouns to a minimum. They're simply not necessary – every reader will know that *your* CV is a document about *you*.

Let's take a simple statement written in the first person as an example:

I possess excellent interpersonal, communication and negotiation skills. I am able to work well on my own initiative and I can demonstrate the levels of self-motivation needed to meet my tightest deadlines.

If you convert this to the third person and strip out the pronouns you get:

Possesses excellent interpersonal, communication and negotiation skills. Able to work well on own initiative and can demonstrate the levels of self-motivation needed to meet the tightest of deadlines.

This is the style in which you should be aiming to write your CV.

As always with CVs, there is no rule which applies 100 per cent of the time and, if you really struggle to word them in the third person, then you can use the first person for your *Professional Profile* and for your *Objective*. But you should categorically stick to the third person for your *Career History*.

Action verbs

We've now covered how to use verbs. Now let's address which verbs you should be using.

An effective way of making your CV have a greater impact is to start your sentences with what are commonly known as 'action verbs'. These are words such as:

> ➤ achieved
> ➤ accomplished
> ➤ developed
> ➤ launched
> ➤ managed
> ➤ maximised
> ➤ strengthened
> ➤ improved
> ➤ implemented
> ➤ realised.

I have included a much more comprehensive list in Appendix A: 250 action verbs – just in case you are struggling to find exactly the right word for your particular circumstances.

These words can be used to describe your skills and experiences in such a way as to emphasise what you achieved rather than just what you did.

Choose your action verbs carefully so that they are as relevant as possible to the role for which you are applying.

The words in my list are all in the past tense. You can of course easily convert them to the present tense if you're writing about your current job, e.g. 'developed' becomes 'develops'. However, this can make for awkward reading. Your best bet is to use what is known as the present 'participle', e.g. 'developing'.

Positive adjectives

You will also want to use a good spread of positive adjectives to help reinforce your statements. Here are some examples:

> ➤ consistent
> ➤ efficient
> ➤ experienced

- innovative
- positive
- productive
- proficient
- resourceful
- successful
- versatile.

And I have included a much more comprehensive list in Appendix B: 50 positive adjectives.

Accompanying adverbs

I should also point out that many of these positive adjectives can be converted to adverbs where necessary, e.g. *successful* becomes *successfully*, *consistent* becomes *consistently*, etc.

Avoiding repetition

Although it can be difficult, you should try hard to avoid repetition in your CV.

This is especially the case with the starting words of bullet points, e.g. developed, implemented, etc. because this always stands out more to the eye than other repetition. Within any one list of bullet points, try to start each bullet point with a different word. Within any one paragraph, avoid using the same adjective, adverb or action verb twice.

Jargon

Feel free to highlight your knowledge and understanding of your work by using relevant terminology and 'buzzwords' – but this should not be overdone.

Excessive jargon is not recommended, particularly since CVs may initially be reviewed by a central HR (human resources) department whose staff may quite simply not understand a lot of the jargon specific to your role.

Numbers

Numbers often speak more than words. Wherever possible you should aim to qualify your statements with specific figures if you really want to maximise the impact. Using qualifying adjectives such as 'major', 'substantial' and 'significant' is all very well but do try to quote precise figures, percentages, etc. if at all possible. Don't just make a claim – back up that claim.

For example, you could say:

Directly responsible for supervising a regional team of Sales Executives.

However, it's always going to be more impressive to say:

Directly responsible for supervising a regional team of 24 Sales Executives.

Always quantify, where possible, whether it's simple figures, percentages or pound notes:

Led the introduction of a major culture change in customer service, improving customer satisfaction ratings from 6.2 out of 10 to 8.3 out of 10.

Personally responsible for delivering the highest sales contribution for the group of 24.4%, with the closest rival delivering just 15.8%.

Successfully tendering for a £2.3 million refurbishment project with a healthy 15% profit margin.

Publishing convention often dictates that the numbers one to ten be written out in full in text, whereas figures should be used for any number higher than that. For example, you can say 314 but you have to spell out seven. This convention is fine for general publishing and is commonly observed in books, magazines and newspapers. However, your CV is not a normal piece of writing; it is a marketing document – and, in marketing, the normal rules don't necessarily apply. I would personally recommend quoting all numbers in figures rather than letters because they're a lot more eye-catching that way and are likely to achieve a greater impact.

Percentages: it is also a common publishing convention for the symbol % to be written as 'per cent'. Again, I would advise against this for the same reasons. A % symbol takes up less space and yet has greater visual impact.

Money, money, money: when it comes to specifying quantities of money, it is accepted practice to abbreviate thousands to the letter K, e.g. £45,000 to £45K. Millions can be similarly abbreviated, e.g. £2.3M, but this is less common and I personally feel that, in this particular case, the full word, 'million' has more of a psychological impact.

Spelling, typos and punctuation

STATISTIC

Sixty per cent of CVs and cover letters contain at least one linguistic error.

For documents which are supposed to be perfect, that's a fairly staggering proportion isn't it?

It is impossible to stress enough how important this issue is. Spelling and grammatical errors are among the most irritating errors a recruiter sees, among the most damaging errors you can make – and are also among the most easily avoided. The answer is to check, check and check again – and then have someone else check for good measure!

Reading through your CV yourself is clearly essential, but having a friend or colleague read through it can be an even better idea – because it's so easy to miss mistakes in your own work when you've been staring at it for hours.

Spelling

Spelling errors can make a huge difference to your career prospects.

In one unfortunate case, the individual in question got very confused about the difference between 'role' and 'roll'. He kept referring throughout both his CV and his cover letter to the various 'rolls' he had had, e.g. 'an important roll in the finance department', 'sharing a roll with another colleague', etc.

BLOOPER!

• •

Another interesting example was the receptionist who spent all day receiving and transmitting massages!

Commonly misspelled words

Any word can be misspelled, even 'misspelled' itself! However, some words are very frequently misspelled in CVs and these are the ones you should keep a particularly careful eye out for:

> separate – often seen spelled as 'seperate'

> necessary – neccesary, necessery, nesessary

> liaising – most commonly misspelled as 'liasing'

> liaison – likewise misspelled as 'liason'

> personnel – personnell, personell, personel.

Easily confused words

There are also various 'pairs' of words which I commonly see used incorrectly in CVs and cover letters, that I'd like to draw to your attention. It can be a little complicated so, if you get at all confused, I suggest you get out the dictionary!

principle/principal

'The principal problem you might face with a new project is that you don't agree, in principle, with the approach the management wants you to take.'

'Principle' is a noun, commonly referring to a personal belief or conviction, e.g. 'It's against my principles.' Alternatively, it can refer to how something works, e.g. 'The principle of a hot air balloon is very simple.'

'Principal', however, can be both an adjective and a noun. As an adjective, it normally means first, main or chief, e.g. 'My principal objection is the cost.' As a noun, however, it has a whole host of different meanings.

stationery/stationary

'You might be responsible for ordering stationery supplies from the stationer. However, if you're stuck in your car at the traffic lights then you're stationary!'

'Stationery' is a noun for writing materials – paper, pens, etc. 'Stationary' is an adjective which means not moving or standing still.

complement/compliment

'If you and a colleague successfully complete a project together then you might compliment each other on a job well done. Alternatively, if he possesses certain skills that you don't – and vice versa – then you might say that you complement each other.'

The two words have very different meanings.

arise/arouse

'A rude and abusive call centre worker could easily cause customer complaints to arise – and that might arouse a rather angry response from the management.'

Again, two words with different meanings.

BLOOPER!

••

'Swiftly and effectively resolving any customer complaints which might arouse.'

effect/affect

'You can effect a change and, depending on the circumstances, you can also affect a change. However, while a change will have an effect, it can't have an affect. And, while you might be affected by a change, you certainly can't be effected by it.'

This is a complicated one!

advice/advise

'You might advise your clients not to sue the local newspaper but they might decide to totally ignore your advice.'

'Advice' is a noun and 'advise' is a verb. They're not only different words; they're also pronounced differently.

practice/practise

'You can work in a doctor's practice and you can put your ideas into practice but if you want to deliver an outstanding presentation to a potential client then you had better practise!'

Whilst pronounced the same, 'practice' is a noun and 'practise' is a verb.

In American English, 'practise' doesn't actually exist at all. Americans use 'practice' both as a noun and a verb and this is just one of many differences between British English and American English.

Let's take a closer look at the vagaries of our American cousins.

Across the pond ...

The differences between British English and American English are numerous and often cause confusion.

The bottom line is that if you're looking for work in the UK, clearly you should be using British English spelling.

We've covered 'practice'/'practise'. Here's another problematic pair:

licence/license

'Licence' is a noun in British English and 'license' is a verb. A driving examiner can license you to drive – but the plastic card you'll get is your licence. Americans, on the other hand don't use the word 'licence' at all. They use 'license' both as a noun and as a verb.

A particular problem is that word-processing software (for example, Microsoft Word) is often, by default, set to American spelling rather than British English (because the software creators are normally American). It will therefore highlight some words as incorrect even when they're not – they're just British English spellings and not American spellings. This can in fact often be resolved by ensuring that the document is set to UK spelling.

TOP TIP

In Microsoft Word 2007:

> Open your CV.

> Select the entire document by pressing Control and A.

> Click on the language bar at the bottom of the screen (next to the Page and Word counts).

> Select English (United Kingdom).

> Click the Default button and tell it 'Yes' so as to update your 'Normal' template (as Word likes to call it).

> Click OK.

The procedure in Microsoft Word 2000/2003 is very similar except that there isn't a language bar. Instead you will need to go to Tools, then Language and across to Set Language. Also, the language will be referred to as 'English UK' rather than 'English (United Kingdom)'.

For other word-processing packages you can consult the user guide or use the built-in 'Help' facility. Failing that, you can find the solution online.

Fully capitalised words

Fully capitalised words are also a problem – because spell checks commonly ignore these. However, this is in fact only the default setting and can be changed.

> **TOP TIP**
>
> **In Microsoft Word 2007:**
>
> ➤ Click on the 'Review' tab.
> ➤ Click 'Spelling & Grammar'.
> ➤ Click Options.
> ➤ Uncheck the box next to 'Ignore words in UPPERCASE'.
> ➤ Click OK.
> ➤ Click Cancel.

The procedure in Microsoft Word 2000/2003 is very similar except that there isn't a 'Review' tab. Instead you will need to go to Tools, then Options, then Spelling & Grammar.

You also need to be careful with acronyms, e.g. BBC, IEEE, CPID, FTP, etc.

Typos

'Typos' or typographical errors can be even harder to pick up on than plain spelling errors. A spell check won't pick up on mistakes such as 'working in a busty office'! You may be surprised, but this sort of error is not unusual. Take a look at where the letters 't' and 'y' sit on a keyboard – right next to each other. It's very easy to try to hit a 'y' and get a 'ty' instead.

As well as adding in an extra letter, another common typo is to completely miss out a letter: 'worked closely with the Finance Manger'.

BLOOPER!

....

I've certainly seen some interesting job titles ... I had one client who was a *Metal Health Advisor* and another who was looking for work as a *Diary Farmer*!

It is not only essential to run a spell check through the finished CV but also to carefully proofread it.

And it's not just words – it can be numbers too:

1881–1995:   BA (Hons) English Literature

That's a very long time to be a student!

Superfluous spaces

You should also be careful to eliminate all superfluous spaces between words, for example 'eliminate   superfluous spaces' has two spaces between 'eliminate' and 'superfluous'.

Word-processing software will often, depending on what type and settings you've got, help you by highlighting such errors (often with green underlining).

Freudian slips

A final type of spelling/typing error I'd like to cover is where the writer, for whatever reason, simply picks the wrong word.

These can be of the banal sort where you type 'their' instead of 'there' or 'your' instead of 'you're'. You know which is correct but your brain somehow sends a different message to the keyboard.

Alternatively, typos can be rather more interesting! One which immediately springs to my mind is the hopeful jobseeker who stated she was 'a conscious employee'. You'd hope so, really...

You probably think I'm making all of this up but, trust me, it wouldn't be in this book if I hadn't actually seen it!

A spell check won't detect these sorts of problem – but a prospective employer very possibly will.

Again, careful proofreading is the answer.

Punctuation

Errors in punctuation are the most common grammatical errors and, among these, the apostrophe is definitely the most abused, for example:

Londons' No. 1 retailer of kitchen appliances.

Or, possibly even worse:

Londons No. 1 retailer of kitchen appliances.

The correct usage is of course:

London's No. 1 retailer of kitchen appliances.

If you're not sure what the rules are then there are plenty of articles on the Internet which explain correct punctuation in detail.

It's and *its* are also frequently misused. And you sometimes even see *its'* – which doesn't exist at all!

Remember that '*it's*' is a contraction of '*it is*' whereas '*its*' is a possessive pronoun, e.g. 'When it's necessary, the computer will automatically update its anti–virus software.'

Poor old apostrophes – so frequently mistreated. The plural of CV isn't in fact even CV's. It should be CVs. However, even some of The CV Centre's competitors get this wrong on their websites!

It's not always black and white of course. Whilst it is grammatically correct to say 'four years' experience', we find a lot of our clients initially complain when we do this, thinking it's an error! Many people assume it should be 'four year's experience'. You might fear (and reasonably so) that a recruiter may also think it is a mistake and so it is better for you to make a deliberate error. The choice is yours. This is the only time I would ever consider recommending anything less than grammatical perfection!

Open and closed punctuation

You will (or certainly should) be using a lot of bullet points in your CV so I'd like to clarify an important punctuation issue specific to bullet points.

Bullet points do not need full stops at the end ('closed' punctuation) unless they are actual grammatically correct sentences (which they generally won't be).

> *This is a bullet point.*

This is obviously a full sentence and so ends with a full stop.

However, most bullet points will read along the lines of:

> *Successfully implementing new procedures leading to a capacity increase exceeding 30%*

This is not a full sentence and so doesn't need a full stop at the end.

Can you spot any spelling, grammatical or typographical errors in this book? We hope not! But, if you do, then please visit **http://www.ineedacv.co.uk/oops** to let us know so we can correct it for the next edition.

Can I leave things out of my CV?

This is a common question I get asked and the answer is not only that you can leave things out of your CV but that you most certainly *should* leave certain things out of your CV.

One incongruity I remember concerns a client, rather high up in the banking world and with a PhD, who insisted on both his O-levels (plus grades) and information regarding his captaincy of the school cricket team (quite a few decades ago ...) being included.

He was clearly an extreme case, but most of the CVs I see contain unnecessary clutter in one form or another.

Look at each piece of information which could be included in your CV and ask yourself, 'Does this help to support my case?' If it doesn't then leave it out. You are under no obligation whatsoever to include everything in your CV.

For a start, in most instances you can eliminate what a prospective employer might see as unnecessary detail – for example only list years, not months within your *Career History* – and this also helps to cover up any chronological gaps. (Medical professions are an exception.)

Concentrate on your recent history and summarise older information. If you've got A levels then don't list all your GCSEs/O-levels. Similarly, if you've got a degree, there's generally no need to include A-level grades unless there's a particular reason to do so, e.g. they're all A or B grades. Employers are most interested in what you've done most recently, although they generally still need to know the basics of older information.

The truth, the whole truth ...

A large percentage of people seem to think it's permissible to tell a few small porkies when writing their CV. Many think it's acceptable because 'everyone else does it' – and it is a fact that many prospective employers do not check an applicant's information as thoroughly as they perhaps should. However, I would always strongly caution everyone against telling anything but the truth on their CV.

Besides the moral aspect, any inaccuracies on a CV can give an employer grounds to dismiss an employee immediately for 'gross misconduct' – and employers do have ways of checking up on you.

BLOOPER!

In one case, it was discovered that a well-known executive, who in every other respect was doing a fine job, had lied about the university degrees he had obtained. He was promptly fired on the spot, getting himself subjected to international media coverage. I was invited onto Sky News to discuss the case and I made the same point then that I will make now: Don't even think about risking it!

You could even become unstuck during the interview, before you even get offered the job. One candidate claimed to be fluent in French on his CV and then got quite a shock when he came up against a half-French/half-English interviewer who consequently thought it quite reasonable to conduct the interview in French!

And, even before the interview, it's not going to do your nerves much good to be worrying about whether or not you are going to be unmasked as a liar. This is a surprisingly common cause of pre-interview jitters.

But doesn't everyone do it?

It all depends, of course, on how you define 'lie'. Twenty per cent engage in a 'significant' lie (the kind where you could be sacked for gross misconduct as a result) whereas up to 35 per cent include at least one small porky here or there.

But just because 'everyone else does it' it doesn't mean that you should. Not everyone lies on their CV – it remains a minority – and it is very questionable whether those that do lie gain any benefit from it whatsoever.

Whether or not you tell the 'whole' truth, though, is another matter entirely. You are under no obligation to include every detail of your life history within your CV and any information which could be perceived negatively should, generally, be omitted or excluded. Examples include being fired from a previous job.

Clearly you should always put as positive a spin as possible on the contents of your CV but it's a fine line – and only you can really be the judge of what is and is not acceptable.

I once read a CV which proudly declared the candidate had worked as a 'Freelance Importer', importing 'various types of merchandise into Jordan – exotic animals, motorbikes, guns, etc.'.

Mentioning that you imported arms into the Middle East is unlikely to be well received by the reader, unless of course that is the line of business you are in. (Incidentally, in this particular case, the candidate was applying for work as an Office Manager ...)

Graduates seem to be particularly prone to 'inaccuracies' on their CVs, the worst errors including deliberately falsifying the class of their university degree.

Deliberately falsifying your degree class is definitely not recommended. However, you can of course simply be economical with the truth, e.g. only list your degree class if it is a 1st or a 2:1.

Chapter **3**

Structure: which type of CV is right for you?

In the first couple of chapters I have covered general principles which could apply to almost anybody setting out to write a CV. Now we need to make a decision as to what specific structure of CV you should use – and there's not one, single correct way to do this. Readers of this book will range from school leavers right the way up to senior executives, and the way you structure your CV will depend very much on your own personal circumstances.

First of all, let's define what are generally seen as the two main types of CV structure that you can use.

Chronological and functional CVs

The two main CV types are: chronological (or reverse chronological, to be precise) and functional.

The chronological CV lists your employment (and academic) history beginning with the most recent and working backwards, with a brief description under each position. This is by far the most widely used.

The functional CV lists your experience under different functional areas, such as Marketing or Customer Service, for example, and this forms the main core of the CV. It focuses on specific skills rather than a full history (making it appropriate for those with a very varied career history). It will include a *Key Skills* section and it will use a *Career Summary* instead of a full *Career History*.

The mixed CV

These two principal types, between them, give rise to a third type, known as the mixed or hybrid CV. A hybrid CV is quite simply a mix of the chronological and functional types. It lists skills/experience under different functions at the top of the CV and then goes on to list previous positions in reverse chronological order.

Other CV types

You may have heard other terms such as an 'inventory CV' and 'targeted CV' but these terms are not in very common use and it is best to focus on the three types I describe above.

Which to use?

The question we really want to answer is which style of CV will generate the most interviews.

STATISTIC

We have conducted careful surveys of our clients and our findings clearly demonstrate that functional CVs simply do not work as well as chronological CVs in terms of winning interviews – at least not in the majority of cases. If they don't get interviews then they shouldn't be used; it's as simple as that.

Recruiters will often bin functional CVs, as they need to see exactly what the candidate has done and where, to really ascertain if they are suitable for the vacancy. There is also the tendency to think that those sending a functional CV are trying to bury or hide something, or want the recruiter to think that they have more experience than they actually do have.

Not all recruiters are the same of course, but the majority aren't particularly fond of the functional CV. Job hunting being a numbers game, it consequently pays to cater to the majority view. However, you should be aware that some recruiters, having received a chronological CV, will then want to see a functional CV as well – especially for senior executive positions.

And not all candidates are the same either. Occasions where a functional CV might be more appropriate include those with very little practical work experience, those seeking to move out of one line of work and into another, for example from military life to civilian life, or those whose professions cause them to change job/contract particularly frequently. We'll cover various special cases such as these in Chapter 13, 'Ten solutions for ten potential problems' and Chapter 14, 'Special cases – professions where the rules are different'.

The mixed type can also be appropriate for certain cases. Many of you may see it as offering the best of both worlds and it is certainly an increasingly popular structure to use.

Section order

Another key structural decision to make is whether to list your *Education and Qualifications* before your *Career History* or vice versa.

It all depends on what is your greater selling point. You should make sure that all your most important information is conveyed on the first page or, for a one-page CV, in the top half of the page.

Which do you feel is most likely to be of interest to a prospective employer? Your *Education and Qualifications* or your *Career History*?

If you've just graduated and have little work experience then clearly your *Education and Qualifications* section is going to be of much greater interest. However, if you left school 40 years ago then it is obviously your *Career History* which is going to be more important to a recruiter.

Even if you only have a little work experience, if you are only qualified to GCSE level you may still feel that your *Career History* is the greater selling point and that you should lead with that rather than your *Education and Qualifications*. It's your call. It's all about conveying the most important, most relevant and most powerful information first.

Depending on your circumstances you may have a whole range of 'additional' sections to include within your CV – *Publications, Research*, etc. Again, you'll need to give careful thought to the order in which you present them. Order them logically and according to the value they contribute.

Reverse chronological order

It is a standard convention on CVs to use reverse chronological order, i.e. to present your most recent information first, followed by older – and consequently less relevant – information. And I would strongly suggest you make sure your CV conforms to this.

Many people find this illogical and don't feel comfortable with the idea. But look at it this way:

Should the first job you ever did really be the first thing a prospective employer sees when looking at your *Career History*? If you're now a Managing Director, then your first job is probably going to look a tad irrelevant. And when they look at your *Education and Qualifications* what should they read first? Details of the GCSEs you sat ten years ago? Or details of the MA in Applied Communication that you've just completed?

It's obvious isn't it?

TOP TIP

....

CVs should always be written in reverse chronological order – the most recent, and therefore most important, items within a section coming first.

Reverse chronological order only applies to the individual entries under each section, not to the order of the sections themselves. We've already established that whether you should 'lead' with *Education and Qualifications* or whether you should lead with *Career History* depends on various different factors. The basic principle is the same though: it's all about conveying the most important, most relevant and most powerful information first.

Length

I have seen CVs over 30 pages long (true!) with photocopies of all their certificates on top of that.

This is not an autobiography you're writing. It's a curriculum vitae. It's a lot shorter!

I always advocate a one-page CV if it is feasible – and some recruitment agencies, especially head-hunters, may insist on a one-page CV.

Failing that, two pages is entirely acceptable and, in certain circumstances, it may be acceptable for a CV to run to three or more pages, but only for certain special cases, e.g. medical, engineering, etc. These are the exceptions that prove the rule – and we'll be covering them in greater detail later in the book under Chapter 14, 'Special cases – professions where the rules are different'.

People often feel that a one-page CV is worth less than a two-pager, but this is definitely not true. It is much better to have a good, strong one-page CV than a two-page one that is padded out with unnecessary information. You should always be aiming to exclude irrelevant information which may detract from other more important points.

Often a CV which has been spread out over two pages can, with a little careful tweaking, be made to fit onto one page – and this tends to have greater impact. It is of course important not to force a CV unnecessarily onto one page when two pages would be better but a 1½ page CV tends to look incomplete and weak.

Regardless of the length, as I said previously, do make sure that all your most important information is conveyed on the first page or, for a one-page CV, in the top half of the page – because too many recruiters simply won't bother to look any further.

What if your finished CV is more than two pages long?

There's only one answer to this question – unless you are a 'special case' you need to keep working on your CV until you've reduced it to the standard two pages.

Take a long, hard look at your CV and consider:

> Removing some of the less important points you've made.

> Finding ways to communicate the same points more concisely.

> Ruthlessly eliminating all unnecessary words and phrases.

> Axing non-essential sections, for example your *Objective*.

> Placing your *Interests and Activities* under *Other Details*.

> Changing the design and page layout to create more space.

> Editing, rewriting, polishing and perfecting until it fits!

Summary

> The very first step you should take in creating your CV is to stop to think for a moment about how you are going to present it. First impressions are absolutely vital.

> Write your CV in the third person and try to keep your use of all pronouns to a minimum. They're simply not necessary.

> Spelling and grammatical errors are so irritating to a reader – yet so easily avoided. Check, double-check and, for good measure, have someone else check too.

> Whilst in most cases I would recommend the chronological CV, you need to be aware of the circumstances in which a functional or hybrid CV would suit you better.

> CVs should always be written in reverse chronological order – the most recent, and therefore most important, items within a section coming first.

PART 2

BUILDING YOUR CV: SECTION BY SECTION

Chapter **4**

Personal details

We've now discussed the general principles of aesthetics, presentation and content, and also established which type of CV is most appropriate for you.

Building on that, this and the following chapters will take each of the principal sections you may include in your CV and discuss them in detail, one by one. We'll go right the way through your CV, section by section, and I'll show you how to configure each section to give you a real winning advantage.

So let's get going.

Personal details

It is vital that the reader can spot, at a glance, not only your name but also precisely how to get in contact with you.

Your CV should be headed with your name – boldly and clearly – before any other details such as contact details, etc. It should not be headed 'Curriculum Vitae' or 'CV' or anything else.

Just your name. And only your first name and your last name.

It is true that, traditionally, CVs were headed with 'Curriculum Vitae', or suchlike, but this convention is very much on the way out now – which is probably a good thing, given how frequently it is misspelled!

BLOOPER!

∙∙∙

One candidate actually headed his CV, 'Kuriculam Vitay'!

Problematic names

I regularly attend recruitment events promoting diversity in the workplace – events which are naturally also attended by a high proportion of individuals of various different ethnic origins. They often ask me questions along the lines of:

> ➤ What if your name is difficult for the average English speaker to pronounce?

> ➤ Do you have to state your 'official' name, i.e. as on your passport?

> ➤ If you're known by a shortened version of your name, then is it alright to use that?

My answer to these questions is that you can – within the limits of common sense – call yourself more or less what you like on your CV. There are no legal restrictions provided you're not attempting to defraud. If you use an alternative, abbreviated or 'anglicised' first name on a regular basis then there's no reason why you can't also use it on your CV. Changing your last name to a shortened version is equally acceptable. The key issue is not to hide your 'real' identity from a prospective employer. When the time comes to deal with contracts of employment you should make them fully aware of your full, official name.

Another popular question is, 'What if it's not obvious from my first name what my gender is?'

The answer's simple. You can of course include your title (Mr, Mrs, etc.) on your CV before your first name. There is certainly no harm in this if it is necessary to clarify your gender. You can also do the same on any cover letters you write.

Your key contact details

You should follow your name with your key contact details. How to present these details? It's much more aesthetically pleasing (and looks a whole lot more professional) to present these as a letterhead, rather than in a list like a form. It also saves a lot of valuable space.

Simply head the CV with your name and follow it with your address and other contact details – address, phone number, email address, etc. Place your address on one line with your phone numbers on the next and finish with your email address.

Addresses

It is generally unnecessary to include UK county names in an address. Royal Mail approved addressing never uses county names. It can be useful though if you are applying for work a long way from where you currently live (if, for example, you are planning to relocate) and you feel that the organisations to which you are applying probably won't be able to work out where you are currently living from the name of your nearest town alone.

It should be noted that there is no need for a comma between city names and post codes.

Telephone (and fax) numbers

Phone numbers should always include the local area code. The correct spacing (according to British Telecom) is, for London, Belfast, etc. 020

7946 0000. For elsewhere it's 01632 960 960. This separates the code out and makes the remainder easier to read.

If you are stating more than one phone number then it's a good idea to specify what each number is, for example, 'Tel: 01632 960 960 (Home); 07700 900 900 (Mobile)'. If you're only including one number then there's no need.

If you're based in one country and your prospective employer is based in another country, then you should endeavour to include international dialling codes with your phone and fax numbers.

I would suggest you avoid using a work telephone number. Even if your current employer knows you are looking elsewhere and is happy for you to use your work telephone number for this purpose, your prospective employer doesn't know this and might think it indicates a lack of respect. A mobile number is normally very much better. It also gives any interested parties one single number on which they can reach you 24 hours a day, 7 days a week.

Email addresses

Whilst not having an email address at all on your CV is clearly a problem, it's not something I see very often. Far more common is the use of fun or jokey email addresses.

Whilst these may be fine for corresponding with friends and family, employers will probably regard more 'serious' email addresses as simply more professional.

Many recruiters report seeing inappropriate email addresses on CVs – and this doesn't do the candidates any favours. Think about what your email address says about you. Email addresses such as sexylady@example.com and hunkyjoe@example.com or, getting really risqué here, mistressdominatrix@example.com and wickedandwild@example.com, will clearly not help you to present a professional image. [By the way, I haven't completely invented these email addresses; I have adapted them from real email addresses I've seen on CVs and have just changed them slightly to protect the innocent! Or not so innocent. ...]

You might have the perfect CV, but if your email address is mrluvverman@example.com then it may harm your chances. I would suggest you open a new email account to use for professional purposes (e.g. Hotmail or Yahoo) and keep your professional correspondence separate from your personal correspondence.

Convention dictates that email addresses should not be capitalised. Aesthetically it's probably more attractive to keep them in lower case anyway.

I'd also like to add that you should make sure that your email address doesn't appear as a 'hyperlink' in your CV, i.e. in blue, underlined text.

Whilst this could arguably be useful in certain circumstances, it can also mean that the email address doesn't print properly to a black-and-white printer – and that is clearly a significant problem. In Microsoft Office you can remove a hyperlink by simply right-clicking on it and selecting 'Remove Hyperlink' from the menu that pops up.

Finally, I would suggest you avoid using a work email address, for the same reasons that you should avoid using a work telephone number. And if your current employer doesn't know you are looking elsewhere then don't forget that they are legally permitted to monitor all of your use of their computer facilities. They're not paying you to hunt for another job!

CASE STUDY

Jane's personal email address is jumpingjane@example.com so she decides it would be best to open a new email account just for her professional correspondence: janebloggs@example.com. Her finished letterhead looks like this:

JANE BLOGGS

1 Any Road, Anytown AN1 1CV
Telephone: 01632 960 960 (Home); 07700 900 900 (Mobile)
Email: janebloggs@example.com

Date of birth

I often get asked whether or not you should include your date of birth (or age) on a CV. The old answer to this used to be that you should include it, because recruiters expect to see it and so if you don't include it then it'll just draw attention to the fact.

However, this advice has now changed – since the introduction of the Employment Equality (Age) Regulations 2006. And, besides, any recruiter worth his or her salt will be able to deduce pretty accurately exactly how old you are just by looking at your education, qualifications and experience.

There is also a security (identity fraud) risk involved in volunteering this sort of highly personal data to all and sundry. Should your CV fall into the wrong hands, this is precisely the sort of information an identity fraudster needs to clone your identity.

Marital Status: SINGLE. Unmarried. Unengaged. Uninvolved. No commitments.

Yes, one individual really did put the above on his CV!

My clients often feel that it is compulsory to include details such as their marital status, nationality, number (and ages) of children/dependants, etc. While, yes, it certainly used to be the norm to include this sort of information on a CV, it is now increasingly rare, given modern anti-discrimination legislation, to find these sorts of details on a CV. They simply aren't relevant.

Too many candidates get too personal. A recruiter does not need to know whether or not you're married, how many children you have, where you like to go on holiday, what your partner's name is, what you normally have for breakfast ... These facts should not affect whether or not you can do the job! They simply clutter up your CV, making it harder for the recruiters to get to the key information that they really need to see.

I have seen a whole range of irrelevant personal information on CVs: maiden name, partner's occupation, even religious belief. I've seen CVs that include totally superfluous details such as National Insurance number, passport number and place of birth. Yes, your employer will eventually need to know your National Insurance number – but not at this early stage. And they should never need to know your place of birth.

BLOOPER!

Other more extreme cases I have seen have included candidates detailing their:

> Height – *I am 6 foot 5 inches tall.*
> Weight – *I weigh 18 stone.*
> Shoe size – *I take a size 10 shoe.*
> Complexion – *Fair (wheatish).*

The only circumstances in which you would normally provide this sort of information is if you're in acting, modelling, etc. (and, needless to say, none of the individuals who put the details above on their CVs were in any way connected to acting or modelling).

One lovey-dovey young couple, looking for work as live-in domestic help, went so far as to proclaim on their CVs that they had to work together because they were 'inseparable soul mates: old souls reunited again from a distant past' (probably late 1960s Haight Ashbury!). They went on to express their 'love of children'. Would you let people like that loose anywhere near your offspring?!

Identity fraud

Besides being entirely superfluous to the recruitment process, including certain personal details will expose you to an increased risk of identity fraud.

STATISTIC

As many as 50 per cent of all CVs contain a sufficient quantity of personal data to enable an identity fraudster to successfully apply for a credit card.

The most useful information to a fraudster includes your name and full postal address in conjunction with your date of birth. Marital status is also very useful.

Many people, however, seem determined to include all sorts of other information which could only really be useful to a fraudster, for example place of birth and passport number. Each individual piece of information is fairly harmless but, collectively, they provide a perfect opportunity for a fraudster to clone and abuse your identity.

Too few people realise the potential consequences if the personal information contained within their CV were to fall into the wrong hands.

Chapter **5**

Professional profile

So, what exactly is a *Professional Profile*?

You've probably heard of the term but you may well be unsure as to what it really means.

A *Professional Profile* is a brief statement at the very beginning of a CV which, in the space of a few short lines, conveys to the reader an overall impression of your key personal and professional characteristics. It's essentially an introduction to your CV and should give the readers a compelling overview before they read on in further detail.

Other terms you may have heard include *Personal Profile* and *Career Profile*. The former clearly concentrates more on personal characteristics and the latter on your career and work experience. A well written *Professional Profile* successfully combines the two.

Should you include a *Professional Profile* on your CV?

There are some people who argue that professional profiles should not be included on CVs anymore because they can perhaps come across as being too self-centred and pompous. However, just so long as the majority of recruiters and employers remain in favour of them, I almost always advocate the inclusion of a *Professional Profile* within a CV.

Some people also wonder why a CV needs to have a *Professional Profile* if you have included a similar summary within your cover letter. The answer is simply that the person conducting an interview may not necessarily see the cover letter. It is not uncommon for whoever does the initial sift of CVs to remove them. And organisations using scanning software (see Part 6, 'Digital considerations') will often only scan in CVs, not cover letters.

The *Professional Profile* can be used to effectively summarise your skills and attributes that you will expound in the main body of the CV and they are also very useful for CVs that are specifically targeted towards a certain position, as they can be used to emphasise the essential criteria that you are able to fulfil. It is a key area to consider tailoring for different applications.

A final reason for creating a *Professional Profile* is that the No. 1 question you are likely to be asked at interview is, 'Can you tell me a bit about yourself?' This is a very broad question – and you might consequently be at a loss as to the approach you should take to answer it. If you've taken the time to think through and write a *Professional Profile,* then a lot of the material within it can be recycled and repurposed to help you draft your answer to this question.

How do you write your *Professional Profile*?

Your *Professional Profile* should only be a few lines in length – five to ten – but must spark the reader's interest. If you can't successfully 'pitch' yourself in under ten lines then you risk losing the reader's attention. Be brief – you can highlight examples in later sections. But be persuasive.

Whilst I'm not saying you can't use bullet points, I would generally recommend that you don't. Make a paragraph of it (just one paragraph). Your CV will be packed full of plenty of bullet points; it makes for a nice visual contrast to start with a 'normal' paragraph.

I mentioned back in Chapter 2, 'Content and style: what to say and how to say it', that you should endeavour to write in the third person but, if you really struggle to word your *Professional Profile* in the third person, then it is acceptable to use the first person.

Alternatively, if you do decide you're happier using bullet points then these should definitely be written in the third person. You should also try to keep it down to a maximum of around five bullet points – and aim to use a different style of bullet point graphic than you have used within your *Career History*. Again, variety is the spice of life.

What to say?

I could talk about this subject for hours but the very best way to teach you how to write your own *Professional Profile* is to show you a couple of real life examples:

EXAMPLE

An enthusiastic and self-motivated professional with extensive experience in financial services and investments. A skilled administrator who specialises in identifying and rectifying discrepancies and issues requiring accuracy and attention to detail at all times. Able to demonstrate an excellent working knowledge of the legislation appropriate to working in financial services with the proven ability to ensure full compliance therewith. Possesses excellent interpersonal skills and the ability to communicate concisely and articulately with clients and colleagues alike. Enjoys being part of a successful and productive team while demonstrating strong leadership potential in a highly competitive and demanding sector.

EXAMPLE

A dedicated and compassionate medical professional who specialises in the field of spinal neurosurgery. Able to demonstrate strong clinical expertise with the proven ability to assess and investigate patient symptoms and make appropriate decisions on the most appropriate treatment accordingly. Committed to the field of research and development with the aim of improving standards of medical practice through the use of technological advances. A valuable member, and leader, of a successful multi-disciplinary team who thrives in highly pressurised and challenging working environments.

I'd also like to fire a small selection of adjectives, phrases and expressions at you. I must emphasise that these are only intended to help to get you thinking in the right direction. It's your *Professional Profile*; you need to write it yourself. There is no set formula. But the following brief lists should help your 'brainstorming' efforts:

> dedicated
> enthusiastic
> positive
> proactive
> dynamic
> versatile
> professional
> Enjoys being part of, as well as leading, a successful and productive team.
> Proven track record in developing successful teams that exceed targets and objectives.
> Passionate about delivering an outstanding service while ensuring a commitment to achieving and exceeding targets and business objectives.
> Attentive to detail with a creative and innovative approach to problem solving and strategy development.
> Quick to grasp new ideas and concepts, and to develop innovative and creative solutions to problems.

> Displays excellent problem-solving and interpersonal skills and can communicate concisely at all levels.

> Possesses excellent interpersonal skills and can communicate concisely at all levels from grassroots to board level.

> Utilises exceptional interpersonal skills and communicative abilities to build effective relationships with clients, suppliers and business colleagues.

> A confident communicator who is able to develop positive internal and external relationships.

> Can demonstrate the high levels of motivation required to meet the tightest of deadlines.

> Thrives in a fast-paced, results-driven environment.

A useful trick is to start off by writing a much longer version than you will actually need – including all the thoughts and ideas that spring to your mind. You can then edit it, rewrite it and cut it down until you eventually achieve the desired length. The text you're left with should be concise and powerful, focusing on the sales points that really matter.

To give you an analogy – good writing is a lot like sculpture. You start with a great big block of marble and you steadily chip away at it, bit by bit, until you've created your masterpiece.

Avoiding cliché and superfluous hyperbole

One of my clients once asked me, 'Aren't words such as "dedicated" and "enthusiastic" a waste of time? Would a recruiter call a client and say, "Hey, I've got a CV from somebody who is dedicated and enthusiastic"?'

She does have a point. No, recruiters indeed wouldn't call up a client and proudly announce they've got a CV from someone who claims to be 'dedicated and enthusiastic'. They'd be intelligent enough to plug some of the candidate's more salient features. However, let's turn her question around and ask what a reader would think of a candidate who didn't say they were dedicated, enthusiastic, etc.? 'Enthusiastic' may be a rather over-used word – but it's also one of the very top characteristics employers look for.

It's clearly a fine line that you're going to have to tread, avoiding cliché and superfluous hyperbole. You are going to need to think very, very carefully how to phrase your *Professional Profile*.

CASE STUDY

Let's see how Jane chooses to tackle her *Professional Profile*:

Professional Profile

A positive, proactive and results-driven Sales Manager with a proven track record of profitable business growth through the creation of successful sales and marketing strategies. Experienced in working with leading brands in the competitive food and drink sector, focusing on exceeding customer service expectations, ensuring optimum brand impact. Possesses excellent interpersonal, communication and negotiation skills and the ability to develop and maintain mutually beneficial relationships with key decision-makers.

BLOOPER!

To conclude this chapter, here's a few examples I have seen of precisely how NOT to phrase your *Professional Profile*:

Well keen and up for everything that I'm interested in. Always on the go. Money, money, money! So enthusiastic for selling; it's in me to SELL, SELL, SELL! Able to persuade Eskimos to buy ice! I want a company car; I want to be out there in the field selling. Buying and selling is all I do and all I want to do. I'm going to achieve all my ambitions. From this day on I'm going to be rich. I know I sound up my own **** but sometimes you need to be to make and get yourself what you want for yourself and for the ones you love. I'm very funny, a great laugh. I've been told that I have a unique outlook on life. [We certainly wouldn't disagree with that last comment would we?]

I am a 5'6" tall, stock Christian (yes, I actually do believe in God), dark hair with a goatee, fit and average weight.

I love arranging and planning and managing things. It all has to flow – like a river! I have an excellent track record – although I'm not a horse! [It's generally best to avoid trying to be humorous when writing a CV.]

A girl of bold, extrovert, charming personality with good administration skills – ready to serve the industry.

I will give a job my all as long as it doesn't interfere with my busy social life. My social life is very important to me.

I don't tend to procrastinate, except when the task is unpleasant or when I have to make a decision.

I always like to breathe in pleasant feelings around me ...

Chapter **6**

Objective

A *Professional Profile* is often, but not always, immediately followed by an *Objective* section. The task of the *Objective* section is to explain your preferred career direction and detail what you hope to achieve from your future career.

Should you include an *Objective* on your CV?

As with the *Professional Profile*, I almost always advocate the inclusion of such a section – if space allows, although being only a sentence or two in length there should normally be enough room to squeeze it in.

As I say, it is not normally essential – one could argue that there is plenty of room in the cover letter to cover the same ground. However, as with the *Professional Profile*, don't forget that people reading your CV may not necessarily see your cover letter. Without the benefit of your cover letter it can otherwise be hard for them to deduce from your CV what it is that you're really looking for.

Of course, if you are aiming for a one-page CV but find that it's impossible to achieve – or impossible to achieve without being detrimental to the presentation – then the *Objective* section is one section you can axe to give yourself that little bit of extra room. It is better to have a one-page CV without an *Objective* than it is to have a 1½ page CV with an *Objective*.

However, one important case where an *Objective* really is essential is if your current job isn't relevant to the one you are now looking for. To help to avoid any confusion on the part of the reader, you need to declare your future career intentions right at the beginning of your CV.

How do you write your *Objective*?

The style in which you write your *Objective* should match the style in which you've written your *Professional Profile*. If you've used a paragraph format for your *Professional Profile*, then you should use a paragraph format for your *Objective*. If, on the other hand, you've used bullet points for your *Professional Profile* then your *Objective* should match this. Whilst variety is good, mixing and matching too many different styles can just look sloppy.

Your aim is to let the readers know what sort of position you are looking for – and to give them another little taste of what you might be able to offer.

Ideally you should make reference to the specific job title of the role you wish to apply for – without this appearing contrived. For example, if you are applying in response to a vacancy for a 'Regional Head of Sales – Surrey' then you would be ill-advised to say:

Now looking for a new and suitably challenging role as a Regional Head of Sales for Surrey.

You would be much better off saying, for example:

Now looking for a new and suitably challenging Head of Sales role.

You've made mention of the key 'Head of Sales' words without appearing desperate for this one particular role!

Whilst mentioning specific job titles is often advantageous, be careful not to box yourself into a corner. Being too specific in your *Objective* could damage your chances if what you say you're looking for doesn't quite meet with what the reader thinks they're offering.

What to say?

As with your *Professional Profile*, the very best way for me to teach you how to write your own *Objective* is to show you some real-life examples:

EXAMPLE

Currently looking for a new and challenging role as a QS, one which will make best use of existing skills and experience while enabling further personal and professional development.

Keen to achieve further professional development. Now looking to build on an extensive range of technical skills within a suitably challenging IT management role.

Currently on the market for a new and challenging position within the corporate sector, one which will make best use of experience acquired in privately owned companies while enabling further personal and professional development.

Now seeking a challenging new position, one which will make best use of existing legal knowledge and experience yet enable further personal and professional development. Keen to take up a new position which will allow her further development within the legal arena.

You'll note that you don't just want to say what you're looking for – you want to seize this opportunity to pack in an additional sales pitch. Show the reader you're someone who is keen for a new challenge – keen to progress further. Show some enthusiasm!

CASE STUDY

Here's how Jane handles her *Objective*:

Objective

Having successfully completed a BA (Hons) in Marketing and Advertising, now looking to return to the food and drink sector in a suitably challenging role. Keen to make best use of broad sales experience and strong theoretical knowledge of marketing and advertising.

BLOOPER!

And here are a couple of (real) examples of what you definitely should NOT say:

Although I trained as a solicitor and for the past ten years have developed a successful career in the legal sector, I am bored by it and hence wondered if you might have any other opportunities that may be of interest to me.

My goal was actually to be a psychologist but since I didn't go to university and get a qualification, I'll have to stick to working within PR.

Chapter **7**

Education and qualifications

Whilst not generally as important as the *Career History* section (it depends on the circumstances), the *Education and Qualifications* section is nevertheless a very important section in most CVs.

If you've just graduated and have little work experience, then clearly your *Education and Qualifications* section is going to be of greater interest than your *Career Summary*. However, if you've already been out in the workplace for some time then it's normally your *Career History* that is going to be more important to a recruiter.

Focusing on what matters

I've already explained why, when writing a CV, you should always focus on more recent history and summarise older information. Recruiters will be most interested in what has happened most recently and, conversely, less interested in what came before, although they obviously still need to know the basics of older information.

For example, if you've got A-levels, then don't list all your GCSEs or O-levels on the CV.

And if your qualifications are limited to a handful of O-levels passed in the 1960s, then why mention them at all? They have absolutely no relevance to your current employability and you're under no obligation to include them.

In the same spirit of focusing on what matters, you should always work in reverse chronological order, i.e. start with your most recent qualification and work backwards. To read more about the concept of reverse chronological order please refer back to Chapter 3, 'Structure: which type of CV is right for you?'

Structure

You want to structure this section clearly so you could use bullet points or a table – or maybe a mixture of the two – to lay out the information.

You need to specify:

> The dates you received your qualifications – or attended the relevant institutions.

> Descriptions of your qualifications, e.g. BSc (Hons) Veterinary Medicine.

> What grades/class/marks you achieved – if applicable.

> If deemed sufficiently relevant, the names of the institution(s) in question.

Dates

Dates are normally required. However, if your most recent qualifications go back a long way then it's fine to omit the dates.

Descriptions of qualifications

Make sure that you state the precise, formal title of the qualifications you have gained. For example, maths should always be spelled out in full, i.e. mathematics, rather than abbreviated.

Grades/class/marks

There's not normally any requirement to list grades in full unless they're a major selling point. For example, if you've got a degree then there's no need to include A-level grades unless they're all As or Bs. The reader is going to be far more interested in your degree than your A-levels.

You could see this as simply being concise or you could see this as being economical with the truth. It all depends on your point of view and your own precise circumstances.

TOP TIP

A situation where you can definitely be economical with the truth is when you have a degree but only achieved a 2:2 or a 3rd. It's not going to add anything to your saleability to quote the degree class; the fact that you graduated is a strong enough selling point on its own. Of course, if you got a 1st or a 2:1 then that's a different matter – because that would clearly be a strong selling point.

An exception to these rules would be the legal professions. The sheer competitiveness of the sector means that recruiters may want to look at your academic background in great detail. As such, a legal CV should be very comprehensive in this respect, including full details of institutions attended, grades achieved, etc. at all levels of study.

Institution names

If you have any qualifications gained at university then you should always name the universities concerned. However, unless you previously attended a particularly well-known school or college, it is generally not necessary to provide its name (legal CVs excepted). As with everything else on your CV, if they're not a selling point, leave them out.

If you're not a graduate then by all means list the name of the school or college you most recently attended – but it's not necessary to list the names of all the institutions you attended. Your prospective employer really won't care.

CASE STUDY

Jane summarises her qualifications as follows:

Education and Qualifications	
BA (Hons):	Marketing and Advertising, University of Sussex (2009)
3 A levels:	English, English Literature and French (1997)
10 GCSEs:	Including English and Mathematics (1995)

Further Training

I'd often recommend following the main *Education and Qualifications* section with either a *Further Training* and/or a *Further Skills* section. It does of course depend on whether or not you have undertaken additional training subsequent to your formal qualifications and whether or not you can demonstrate specific additional skills for which you have no formal qualification.

The *Further Training* or *Vocational Training* (or maybe even *Technical Training* or *Continuing Professional Development*) section should make mention of useful classes and courses you have undertaken during the course of your career. Employers place a lot of value on Continuing

Professional Development (CPD); in many professions (medical, teaching, etc.) you are expected to be continually learning. I'm not saying you should necessarily list every class, course, seminar, etc. If you've attended them by the dozen then, as always, focus on those which will be of the greatest interest to a prospective employer.

EXAMPLE

Further Training

- Management Development Programme
- Marketing Management
- Presentation Skills
- Finance for Non-Financial Managers
- Effective Man Management
- Appraisal Training
- Team Building
- Creativity Training

While qualifications such as NVQs are best listed within your main *Education and Qualifications* section, professional qualifications such as the European Computer Driving Licence (ECDL) and the RSA Computer Literacy and Information Technology (CLAIT) qualifications are probably best placed within *Further Training*.

CASE STUDY

Jane has undertaken a couple of valuable courses and lists them as follows:

Further Training

- CLAIT Level 1: Including optional unit in Database Manipulation (2009)
- Commercial Awareness & Marketing Intelligence (2007)

Further Skills

The *Further Skills* section can be used to provide details of IT skills, linguistic skills, etc.

On the subject of IT skills, do ensure you get the names, spacing and capitalisation of IT packages correct, e.g. QuarkXPress, PowerPoint, etc. (this

EDUCATION AND QUALIFICATIONS

65

convention is known as 'CamelCase' or medial capitals, BiCapitalisation, CapWords and InterCaps – and originated within the IT sector, although it has now spread to other areas). If in doubt, check!

CASE STUDY

Following completion of her CLAIT course, Jane has a range of valuable IT skills and, having lived in France for a time, speaks French fluently. She also studied German at GCSE and can still 'get by'.

Further Skills

IT Skills:	MS Office including PowerPoint & Access, QuarkXPress and PhotoShop
Languages:	Fluent French; basic German

Language skills are always of interest to employers and your level should be specified as basic, intermediate/conversational or fluent.

If the only skills you need to highlight within your *Further Skills* section are IT skills then you can simply re-title the section *IT Skills* or *Key IT Skills* and bullet point the list.

EXAMPLE

IT Skills

- MS Office including PowerPoint & Access, QuarkXPress and PhotoShop

However, if your IT skills are very extensive (for example you work within IT) then it's best to make them easier to scan by breaking them down by category, for example hardware, software, programming languages, network protocols, etc.

You should also highlight your accreditation with Microsoft, Cisco, etc.

Other information you could place under *Further Skills* may include details of driving licences if that is of particular importance to your work, for example if you're an HGV driver. However, generally this is best left to the *Other Details* section that we'll come to in a later chapter.

If you are in a non-medical profession and have completed an appropriate First Aid at Work qualification, then you could also include this under *Further Skills*. Or you could just include it under *Other Details* (see Chapter 11, 'Other details'). It's up to you!

Chapter **8**

Career history

The *Career History* section is, in most cases, the most important single section of a CV – the exception of course being those with little or no work experience, for example recent school leavers and graduates.

There are a variety of possible headings for this section that you can use instead of *Career History*. If you feel the word 'career' isn't really applicable to your circumstances – for example if you are a recent graduate and haven't even started your career – then you might prefer to say *Employment History* or *Work Experience*.

Whatever you choose to call the section, the basic principles stay the same.

Focusing on what matters

Just like your *Education and Qualifications*, you should always work in reverse chronological order, i.e. start with your present or most recent job and work all the way back to your very first job.

Again, as with your *Education and Qualifications*, focus more on more recent information and summarise older information. Your current or most recent job should nearly always have the most detail.

Prospective employers are clearly going to be most interested in points that are most relevant to them, so aim to remain concise when describing roles that aren't particularly relevant to the job you are applying for – and, conversely, make sure that you highlight and elaborate on any roles that are indeed relevant.

TOP TIP

If you don't have a one-page CV, then do ensure that at least your current or most recent employment features on the first page of your CV.

And if you're struggling to fit your CV onto the recommended maximum of two pages, then it is very likely that you are putting too much detail into your *Career History*.

Structure

You need to specify:

> The dates you worked for each organisation.

> Your job title or function, e.g. Head of Marketing.

> The name of the organisation you worked for, along with its location.

> A compelling description of what your role entailed.

Dates

Unexplained gaps in your employment record can naturally raise concerns in the minds of recruiters. They may think you have something to hide!

A useful 'trick' I have already mentioned is to cover up brief chronological gaps by only listing years, not months within your *Career History*. I'd recommend doing this regardless of whether or not you have any gaps. I consider listing all the months to be unnecessary detail (although some recruiters, especially some recruitment agencies, may still insist on all the months being listed – and medical professionals should always provide full details).

If you have larger gaps than can be concealed by simply omitting the months then that can be problematic – but there are of course solutions, and we'll cover these later in Chapter 13, 'Ten solutions for ten potential problems'.

And if you're still in the role then you can use the term, 'to date', for example '2007–date'.

Your job title or function

This is fairly self-explanatory. My only word of warning is not to embellish. Remember: your prospective employer may well contact previous employers for references and you don't want your prospective employer to refer to you as a Project Manager when you were in fact just an Assistant Project Manager!

Details of the organisation you worked for

There are only a few different kinds of organisation you are likely to have worked for.

The two most common are a private limited company and a public limited company.

The CV Centre is a private limited company – 'The CV Centre Limited'. In fact, most SMEs (small and medium enterprises) in the UK are private limited companies – and SMEs employ a very large proportion of the country's workforce.

A public limited company, on the other hand, is normally a much larger enterprise, for example Sainsbury's the supermarket – 'J. Sainsbury plc'. Whilst there are far fewer public limited companies than private limited companies, they nevertheless employ a significant proportion of the population because their workforces are generally very large, often tens of thousands.

The 'Limited' part of the name of a private limited company can be abbreviated to 'Ltd.' to save space – but the initial letter 'L' should always be capitalised.

On the other hand, 'plc' (public limited company) should be written in lower case – and should never have a full stop after it.

Technically speaking, plc can also be written PLC (but not Plc) and Ltd. can be written ltd, but Ltd. and plc are the most common usages and therefore probably the best to use.

As regards location, it is sufficient to just list the town or city (and, if abroad, the country). There's no need at all for a full address.

A compelling description of what your role entailed

Not a dry and boring job description! You'd be surprised how many people copy and paste their official job description into their CV. This is most definitely not recommended – especially when the original has spelling or grammatical errors!

This is the most important content in your *Career History* and you have to get it right.

Besides carefully describing your main duties and responsibilities, you should also aim to give specific examples where possible. Including brief but relevant examples as to how you meet your prospective employer's criteria can make a big difference to the credibility of your words.

This is the place to really emphasise what it was that you achieved in each role (bearing in mind that you might also decide to have a separate *Achievements* section – see Chapter 10, 'Achievements').

Pay attention to the order in which you list your bullet points. They should be listed in a logical order, grouping together similar items and – vitally – your greatest selling points should come first. This is another reason for not simply copying your official job description; they frequently focus on what you spend most of your time doing – not what is most important.

TOP TIP

Don't feel you should only include paid, permanent employment. Relevant unpaid or temporary work can be a valuable addition to your CV. It all depends on precisely what it was you did – and how you choose to describe it.

Unnecessary detail

I often see salary details and/or 'reason for leaving' detailed under each job on people's CVs. Don't do this. It's superfluous, unnecessary detail.

Salary is always a sensitive issue. Not only shouldn't you bring it up in your CV but you shouldn't even raise the subject at interview – at least not until a firm job offer is being negotiated. Providing precise details of your salary in advance is inappropriate and can potentially serve to weaken your position when it comes to negotiating the salary package you are now looking for. Unless you have specifically been asked to include such information on your CV, leave it out. If an employer really wants to know details of your salary history they can always ask when they interview you.

Your reasons for leaving a job can also be a delicate matter to handle – and can often be hard to explain concisely. Why take up valuable room on your CV explaining your reasons for leaving when that space could be better spent incorporating additional sales points? Most recruiters won't be expecting your reasons for leaving to be detailed on your CV and, if they really want to know, then the interview is the appropriate time for such issues to be discussed.

BLOOPER!

•••

One young lady really laid into her current employer on her CV, stating what a complete ***** she was and how badly she was verbally abused on an almost daily basis. This was undoubtedly a very unfortunate situation for her – but making an issue of it in her CV was definitely not doing her any favours getting a new job!

Career Summary and Key Experience

Instead of a full *Career History*, you may wish to consider using a *Career Summary*. This is perhaps most appropriate if you have opted for a functional or hybrid CV. (See Chapter 3, 'Structure: which type of CV is right for you?' for a detailed explanation of the different types of CV.)

If you have a long and varied *Career History* and/or are now looking to change career path then the best approach might be to start by writing a 'normal' *Career History* but then divide it up into three separate sections:

> ➤ *Key Experience*
> ➤ *Current Employment*
> ➤ *Career Summary*

This will help to dilute the attention which might be focused on any particular role.

Within the *Key Experience* section you should highlight aspects of your *Career History* that are most relevant to the role you are now looking to undertake, possibly split into separate sub-headings.

The *Current Employment* section can give comprehensive details of your current role – always of interest to a prospective employer.

And the *Career Summary* only needs to list dates, job titles and employers' names and locations – no details of duties, responsibilities and achievements.

EXAMPLE

....

Key Experience

Team Management

- Managing the recruitment and selection process to ensure that appropriately qualified and experienced staff are hired in accordance with business requirements
- Conducting regular staff appraisals and providing constructive feedback to facilitate progression and performance improvements in line with business development plans
- Encouraging all members of staff to support company strategies and initiatives whilst ensuring that they remain focused on providing a world class standard of service
- Coordinating the provision of comprehensive training to all staff to ensure that they have the knowledge and capabilities required to fulfil their job roles to the very best of their abilities
- Adopting a supportive management style that encourages staff at all levels to openly discuss any concerns they may have and working collaboratively to facilitate their resolution

Performance Management

- Chairing and documenting weekly management team meetings to monitor the achievement of KPIs
- Developing and executing innovative strategies designed to achieve increased market share in a competitive industry as well as implementing local and central marketing activities
- Taking appropriate action to resolve any issues identified following a review of internal management systems
- Playing a pivotal role in ensuring that all employees comply fully with company procedures and industry specific legislation
- Completing audits and risk assessments with the aim of ensuring full compliance with health, safety and security guidelines and legislation

Business Management

- Providing a visible management presence for customers and maximising all opportunities to interact with them thereby encouraging repeat business
- Proactively seeking feedback from customers as well as reviewing customer attendance information and taking appropriate steps to drive improvements
- Conducting thorough investigations into any complaints that may arise and providing solutions that are satisfactory to the business and the customer
- Travelling extensively to review performance and standards in company and competitor units and identifying areas for improvement in terms of revenue growth within the unit

Recent Career History and Previous Employment

If you are worried that your age may be counting against you, then the best technique at your disposal is to place the focus very firmly on your most recent history and to radically summarise earlier information.

To achieve this, you can split your *Career History* into a *Recent Career History* section spanning the past decade or so and a *Previous Employment* section. The former can go into appropriate detail but the latter should only list job titles, employers' names and locations – no dates or details of duties, responsibilities and achievements.

Employment History and Work Experience

Even if you have little or no work experience – you may only have worked to help to fund your studies – you should still find it worth mentioning. Some workplace experience is always better than none.

CASE STUDY

Let's look at how Jane describes her current role:

Career Summary

2007–date   Sales Manager, ABC Stationery plc, London
- Playing a key role within a large stationery retailer, tasked with the redevelopment of the sales strategy across the UK market
- Planning and executing innovative campaigns, including direct mail and telesales
- Personally cold calling to bring on board high profile – and credit-worthy – new clients
- Liaising extensively with clients to agree product specifications, sale prices and lead times
- Building mutually beneficial relationships with suppliers, negotiating terms and discounts

She will also be adding some achievements to this but we'll come on to that in Chapter 10, 'Achievements'.

Chapter **9**

Key Skills

So, what is a *Key Skills* section exactly? It's often misunderstood.

A *Key Skills* section is a summary of the main skills and abilities you are offering a prospective employer – your top selling points in terms of skills and abilities.

It shouldn't be confused with an *Achievements* section (which we'll cover in the next chapter). An *Achievements* section will focus on your experience rather than your pure skills and abilities.

Should you include a *Key Skills* section on your CV?

One school of thought is that by including a *Key Skills* section on the first page it's impossible for recruiters to miss it – or at least very hard for them to ignore. However, the inclusion of a *Key Skills* section in a CV is progressively less popular these days. It is now generally considered better to spread evidence of key skills and abilities throughout your career history. This is a more powerful and convincing approach. (You can also address specific points in the cover letter, a vitally important part of any application.)

However, a *Key Skills* section remains essential for the 'functional' CV type.

What to include

Recent school leavers and graduates can pick out skills they've acquired during their studies – regardless of whether or not you've yet had a chance to apply them in the workplace – and feature them as bullet points within a *Key Skills* section.

And if you're adopting the functional CV approach because your previous experience is not directly relevant to the role you are now seeking, then you should make use of the *Key Skills* section to focus on the transferable skills and abilities that you have developed during the course of your career.

If you can, try to break up your key skills under separate sub-headings, grouping together related items in a logical fashion.

For example, you could have different headings for:

> Communication Skills

> Interpersonal Skills

> Administrative Skills

> Organisational Skills

> Negotiation Skills

> Presentation Skills

> Research Skills

> Numerical Skills

This is just a selection of ideas for possible headings rather than a precise formula. You will need to list out all your own skills – bearing in mind the demands of the job for which you are applying – and then seek to categorise them as best suits your own personal circumstances.

Talking of the importance of taking into consideration the requirements of the job for which you are applying, the *Key Skills* section is always an area to consider tailoring carefully for each individual application. While you should be subtle about this – and not simply repeat everything which has been listed in the person specification – you should of course ensure that you cover all the bases.

Key Strengths

An alternative approach which I occasionally see is a *Key Strengths* section. This is often used as a way to combine the *Key Skills* and *Achievements* sections – but it may also be used in addition. Essentially it takes particular skills and abilities and backs them up with evidence and examples. (Many people mistakenly mix up the terms 'Key Strengths' and 'Key Skills' but the difference is clear – a *Key Strengths* section contains a lot more background information.)

My professional opinion is that:

> A *Key Skills* section is generally not necessary (except for functional and 'mixed' CVs).

> An *Achievements* section is generally highly recommended (see next chapter) .

> Any ideas you have for *Key Strengths* would be best placed in your *Career Summary*.

However, as always, there are exceptions to the rules and, depending on your career history and your precise mix of key skills and achievements, you may feel you would be best served by a *Key Strengths* section. It shouldn't take long to knock up drafts of both versions and you can then get a clear idea as to which approach works best for you.

BLOOPER!

• •

I know I've included a lot of real-life examples in this book which defy belief but I promise I haven't invented any of them! You have to bear in mind that I have seen thousands upon thousands of CVs so there are inevitably going to be some really cracking blunders in among them. The following example *Key Skills* section is certainly no exception …

Strengths:

➤ Pretty

➤ Lovely Smile

➤ Nice Puppies

➤ Cute Bum

Weaknesses:

➤ A couple of brown tramlines inside thighs

➤ Inability to frown

I was very tempted to tell the owner of this particular CV that she should perhaps consider writing this in prose instead of bullet points: 'I am a pretty little thing with nice puppies and a cute bum, although I have been told that I have curious brown tramlines inside my thighs.' However, I erred on the side of caution and politely suggested that she might be better off leaving out the section entirely.

For the avoidance of any possible doubt, you should definitely not subdivide your *Key Skills* section into 'Strengths' and 'Weaknesses'. Weaknesses have no place in your CV – it's the strengths we're interested in!

Chapter **10**

Achievements

Including an *Achievements* (or *Accomplishments*) section on a CV is by no means compulsory – and there are many instances where it simply won't apply. But if you can include such a section then it could really make an instant and dramatic difference to the power of your CV. It helps prevent your career history from reading too much like a job description and it gives you an opportunity to distinguish yourself from other candidates.

This is no time for false modesty. This is a time to show what you have achieved – and to imply that you will be capable of achieving similar results in the future.

The one goal of your CV is to get you an interview and this one change to your CV will undoubtedly help to get you noticed, leading to more interview invitations.

'Achievements' is a powerful and positive word and it will immediately convey a powerful and positive impression of you to the reader. It differentiates you as not just another average candidate. Given the competition you are likely to be facing, being average will not get you the job. You have to set yourself apart. So many above-average candidates let themselves down with a below-average CV.

Integrating achievements into your CV

You might choose to have either one collective *Achievements* section in your CV or, if you feel you have enough to say for yourself to warrant it, you can even have separate little *Achievements* sub-headings under each role in your *Career History*. Whichever you choose, it is worth noting that you should be careful to avoid repetition in your CV. If you have something to say then say it once – and once only. Space is always at a premium.

If you do choose to include separate *Achievements* sections under each role then you should still of course include full details of your responsibilities in each role – but place your achievements first. Make sure that your achievements are the first items that catch the reader's eye – because they are the most compelling. If you can include details of achievements then you should place the focus on your achievements, not on your responsibilities. Your responsibilities become of secondary importance.

TOP TIP

A word of warning for more mature candidates: if you have an extensive *Career History* then make sure you limit your entries to recent achievements. Don't go back any further than the past decade or so.

What words to use

You must be economical in your use of words. If you want your statements to have the maximum impact then they need to be concise. Don't pad out your bullet points with superfluous detail and explanations; you'll lose momentum.

You may recall that 'achieved' is one of the 'action verbs' we talked about in Chapter 2, 'Content and style: what to say and how to say it'. Please refer back to this chapter for further ideas on how best to express yourself. You may also like to take a look at 'Appendix A: 250 action verbs', for further ideas.

What are employers looking for?

To help trigger your thought processes, here are some examples of the sorts of contribution employers expect their employees to make:

> Increase: Profits; Sales/turnover; Working capital; Market share; Efficiency

> Decrease: Costs; Waste; Excess stock; Timescales; Complaints; Staff turnover

> Improve: Cashflow; Procedures; Performance; Teamwork; Reputation; PR

> Arrange: Change; Innovation; Events; Results

Think back through your career and identify instances where you have made such contributions.

I have summarised these ideas under just four headings: increase, decrease, improve and arrange. However, you will be able to add diversity to your statements by making use of the broad range of action verbs in 'Appendix A: 250 action verbs'.

Quantify

In Chapter 2, 'Content and style: what to say and how to say it', I also discussed the importance of backing up your claims.

Here are some examples for you:

EXAMPLE

· ·

Delivered a substantial increase in weekly sales levels, from £45,000 to £85,000 – nearly doubling sales

Personally responsible for delivering the highest sales contribution for the group of 24.4%, with the closest rival delivering just 15.8%

Won the Deputy Manager of the Year Award in 2008, resulting in promotion to the management of the flagship Liverpool branch

Successfully drove down stock from £1.5 million to £800K in just nine months while maintaining lead times, consequently boosting working capital by £700K

Increased market share from 12% to 15% over an 18-month period – an increase of 25%

Personally achieved a 34% increase in uptake of after-sales insurance packages

Improved production line procedures, reducing producing time by 12%, raising efficiency and reducing costs

Successfully reducing VAT reconciliation discrepancies from £6 million to just £25K

If you weren't solely and personally responsible for a particular achievement but supported a team or another individual in doing so then don't hold back – you're entitled to credit for it too!

EXAMPLE

· ·

Played a key role within the team responsible for smashing the previous regional sales record by an impressive 37%

Jane thinks back through her career and identifies the following achievements she can include in her CV:

> Led the introduction of a major culture change in customer service, improving customer satisfaction ratings from 6.2 out of 10 to 8.3 out of 10

> Boosted regional sales levels by nearly 35% over a two-year period with no additional marketing spend

> Organised a successful new product launch, gaining a substantial amount of local and national press coverage

> Featured in the programme, 'Business Lunch' on XYZ TV, providing invaluable exposure for the business

Personal achievements can also be important

Besides highlighting achievements from your professional and academic life, you should also consider including personal achievements – as these help to reflect your personality and add that little extra something which will help to differentiate you from your competition. We'll cover personal achievements in greater detail in Chapter 12, 'Interests and activities'.

Chapter **11**

Other details

The *Other Details* section is somewhat of a mixed bag. Use it to make mention of any bits and pieces that don't readily fit into other sections or which aren't sufficiently important to merit inclusion within other sections.

Driving licence

Details of your driving licence, if you have one, should always be included on your CV, even if your licence isn't 'clean'. Under normal circumstances you can describe it as being 'Full/Clean' or 'Provisional/Clean'. However if, you have any points on your licence, then simply describe it as 'Full' (or 'Provisional' if applicable). It's obviously going to be rather negative to list the number of points you have (as some people do). And, naturally, if you've been banned then you should avoid making any mention of your licence (or lack of) whatsoever.

Please note that if driving is vital to your work, for example if you're an HGV driver, then you can 'promote' mention of your licence(s) to a *Further Skills* section.

TOP TIP

Do remember that the correct spelling in the UK is 'licence' and not 'license'.

Health

Should you include details of your health, including, for example, whether or not you smoke?

Well, you certainly shouldn't state that you do smoke or have any health problems on the CV itself – but if your health is excellent and you're a non-smoker then by all means mention that. Only do so if there's space of course. Don't try to force it in if you can think of something more constructive to include.

If you have a recognised disability then the Disability Discrimination Act normally prevents a prospective employer from discriminating against you on these grounds. However, as we all well know, the reality is that some employers will flout the law. I would therefore recommend you wait until you attend interview to disclose any disability or, if your disability is not immediately obvious to an employer when you attend the interview, you can even wait until you receive a firm job offer.

You should note that, whilst employers are not generally allowed to discriminate on the basis of disability, it is nevertheless entirely permissible for them to question you on this subject at interview – because there are certain exceptions to the rules.

First aid

If you're in a medical profession, then it's clearly a little ridiculous to talk about your first aid skills here. However, if you are in a non-medical profession and have completed an appropriate First Aid at Work qualification then *Other Details* is the place to make mention of it. It's all grist to your mill. Alternatively, if you've implemented a *Further Skills* section (see Chapter 7, 'Education and qualifications') you may decide this is the more appropriate place.

Professional registration

Talking of medical professions, the *Other Details* section is the place to provide details of your professional registration, including reference numbers. But don't include details of your hepatitis B status; it's jumping the gun.

Professional memberships

You should highlight any relevant professional affiliations such as membership of the British Computer Society. They're valuable selling points.

Many sectors now offer the opportunity to become a member of a professional organisation – with various different levels of membership achievable – and becoming a member of a professional organisation provides external recognition of your competence.

Nationality

As we've already established in a previous chapter, it's not recommended to include your nationality – due to the risk of discrimination. However, if you are a citizen of a country outside the EU (European Union), then you can highlight your right to work in the UK. It will assuage any concerns a prospective employer may have on this front.

Relocation

If you're applying for a vacancy that is clearly beyond reasonable commuting distance of your current residence, then it can be helpful to indicate on your CV that you are prepared to relocate. In some cases this will be essential, for example a British company might be advertising for someone to oversee their expansion into China, with the successful applicant being based in the Shanghai office.

> **EXAMPLE**
>
> **Relocation:** Prepared to relocate for the right opportunity

Holiday plans

One candidate that came to us for help, having achieved very little success with her own CV, had specified within the *Other Details* section of her CV her holiday plans for the next three years – and made it quite clear that she would not be changing them and that any prospective employer would have to accommodate them! Her annual trips were very important to her.

First of all, imposing these kinds of restrictions on a prospective employer clearly isn't going to be to your advantage. And, secondly, the *Other Details* section of your CV is definitely not the place to communicate this sort of information. It should be saved for the cover letter or, preferably, the interview itself. By that stage you've got your foot in the door and an employer who is keen to have you on board is more likely to make a greater effort to accommodate such stipulations. But don't count on it!

We completely removed all mention of holidays from this lady's CV (and made quite a number of other changes), advised her to raise the issue at interview instead, and she managed to secure a new job within a couple of weeks. Her new employer was prepared to accept her holiday commitments for the year ahead, albeit not the full three years she had insisted upon. Sometimes you have to know when to compromise!

Interests and Activities

We'll be discussing the *Interests and Activities* section of your CV in the next chapter. However, I would just like to mention here that if you aren't planning to include such a section because you don't feel there's enough room then there is an alternative approach. You can simply summarise your interests as one line under *Other Details*, for example, 'Interests include: x, y and z'.

EXAMPLE

Interests include: Badminton, Squash, Pilates, Theatre & Amateur Dramatics, and Cinema

---

Referees

Details of referees generally shouldn't be included on your CV. They're a waste of valuable space! They clutter it up and, more importantly, you will find that your referees get pestered unnecessarily by time wasters. By the time they have handled their umpteenth enquiry of the day, they are a lot less likely to say nice things about you!

A simple statement at the bottom of your CV, saying 'References are available on request' is more than sufficient, because it's not information that a recruiter needs to have up front. When your application progresses to the next level and there is serious talk of a job offer then that is the time to provide these details.

The main exception to this rule is, of course, when you are specifically instructed to provide details of referees with your initial application. Some employers will insist on having details of referees up front – as will some recruitment agencies.

Obviously, if you have been specifically instructed to do so then you have little choice but to comply. However, it's not normally necessary to have to squeeze this extra information into your CV. If you've spent time perfecting the layout of your CV then adding in all this extra information is likely to be quite time-consuming, not to mention detrimental to the impact of your CV. You should instead simply provide full details on a separate sheet – matching in style with your CV of course.

There are other exceptions – medical CVs, for example – and we'll cover these in Chapter 14, 'Special cases – professions where the rules are different'.

Handling convictions

Undoubtedly, a criminal conviction is going to be difficult to handle.

> **BLOOPER!**
>
> Explaining a conviction by simply saying, 'I killed my wife' (yes, you won't believe me, but one candidate famously did put this on his CV), is not going to get you invited to an interview!

The solution is simple – don't make any mention of criminal convictions. You are not under any obligation to disclose convictions unless:

> you are specifically asked to do so.

> you are applying for one of a small number of 'special cases'.

It is important to appreciate that the Rehabilitation of Offenders Act allows for certain criminal convictions to be deemed 'spent' after what is termed a 'rehabilitation period'. If a criminal conviction is spent then you are permitted to conceal it from a prospective employer – with certain exceptions – and if you have any criminal convictions then it is vital to be aware of what this rehabilitation period is.

The Act also makes it unlawful for record-keeping bodies such as the Criminal Records Bureau to disclose details of such convictions.

However, these general rules do not apply to certain employers and organisations. The rationale is to ensure that employers and organisations offering certain sensitive positions, professions and licences can access an applicant's full criminal history before reaching a decision.

If you are in any doubt as regards your own specific circumstances then it's always best to seek appropriate professional advice.

CASE STUDY

Jane's circumstances are very simple. She has a full, clean driving licence and she's a non-smoker in excellent health.

Other Details	
Driving Licence:	Full/Clean
Health:	Excellent; non-smoker

Chapter **12**

Interests and activities

There's always a lot of debate about the *Interests and Activities* section. In this chapter I'll outline the pros and cons of including such a section, explain my opinion on the matter, and also detail precisely how you should handle your own *Interests and Activities* section – if you decide to include one.

Should you or shouldn't you?

Before we discuss what to – or, perhaps more importantly, what not to – include in this section, let's first of all ask ourselves whether or not you should even bother including such a section on your CV.

As with many other aspects of your CV, there are reasons for and reasons against.

First let's look at the reasons *against* including such a section:

> ➤ Space is normally at a premium in a CV. It is vital to prioritise and only include information which will help to make your case. So why include your hobbies and pastimes? Are they relevant?

> ➤ A number of surveys have resulted in comments from recruiters that *Interests and Activities* sections are 'a waste of space' or, worse, 'tiresome and tedious'.

> ➤ A trained recruiter should theoretically totally disregard this section when short-listing – because it's technically of no relevance whatsoever to the candidature and is notorious for including exaggerations and mistruths.

STATISTIC

· ·

An interesting survey by the Recruitment and Employment Confederation found that 71 per cent of recruiters had actually decided not to short-list a candidate purely as a result of information they put under *Interests and Activities*.

Now let's tackle the reasons why you *should* include such a section:

> ➤ Whilst nobody has yet conducted a survey specifically to research this, there is plenty of anecdotal evidence of recruiters deciding to call someone in for an interview purely as a result of what they've

included on their CV under *Interests and Activities*. I, for one, will admit to having done so when hiring.

> We are naturally attracted to people who share our own interests in life, so if your interests match those of the recruiters reading your CV, there is a high probability it will increase your chances of their interviewing you.

> Without an *Interests and Activities* section, a CV can be rather a cold, lifeless document. Including brief details of what you do outside of office hours can bring a much-needed personal touch to a CV.

> Sifting through large piles of CVs can be very tedious indeed, and reading the *Interests and Activities* sections can make the task that little bit more interesting for the recruiter.

> Anything (within reason!) that can help your CV stand out from the crowd and grab the reader's attention could give you an advantage over other potential candidates.

> Whilst saying that you enjoy 'socialising' might well come across as a 'tiresome and tedious waste of space' in the eyes of a recruiter, with a little thought and effort you should be able to come up with some more imaginative alternatives.

> Giving an interviewer the opportunity to talk about your *Interests and Activities* can be an excellent ice-breaker.

> Besides knowing whether you're capable of actually doing the job, most employers are keen to know what sort of a person you would be like to work alongside. Yes, they can get an idea at interview but your *Interests and Activities* can also give them some insight.

> Employers are generally keen to have a diversity of characters within their team and are always on the lookout for someone who can add a new dimension to the team.

So what to conclude?

Yes, I have listed more reasons for including an *Interests and Activities* section than I have listed not to include one. And, for the time being, I remain firmly convinced that you most certainly should include such a section on your CV. But – and this is very important – you most certainly should not go overboard on it. Keep it short. Keep it simple. Don't write a whole essay about what you do in your spare time.

Graduates, in particular, often fall foul on this point, not infrequently devoting up to half an A4 page to their 'extracurricular' activities. Writing far too much under *Interests and Activities* is a common mistake I see. Detailed explanations are best saved for the interview stage. For one thing, you want to avoid giving the impression that your hobbies are more important to you than your career. If a prospective employer fears that your hobbies may well end up taking priority over your work life, then that is definitely not going to count in your favour.

Obviously, information that is directly relevant to the position you are applying for should always take precedence but, space allowing, my professional opinion is that an *Interests and Activities* section rounds off a CV nicely and helps to bring it to life just at the point the reader is about to make that critical decision whether or not to invite the applicant for interview.

STATISTIC

I would warn that statistics reveal a trend over the past ten years of an increasing number of people choosing to omit such a section and so a time may come when this section of a CV becomes history. But, until the majority of job hunters decide not to include their *Interests and Activities*, this is one instance where I would recommend 'going with the herd'.

It's normally far from compulsory though. If you really feel that you have nothing to say in this section (perhaps your work is your life) then naturally you have little choice but to leave it out.

Leaving it out can also be a useful little trick to gain a little bit of extra space on your CV if you're finding it difficult to fit everything else in without it appearing cramped.

Alternatively, you can simply summarise your interests as one line under *Other Details*, for example, 'Interests include: x, y and z' instead of dedicating an entire, separate section to them.

Teachers, however, should bear in mind that extracurricular activities are of particular interest to recruiters. Recruiters will be looking for evidence that you really want to get involved with all aspects of school life, contribute to the community and build relationships with the students both in and out of the classroom. In your case, an *Interests and Activities* section is vital.

What to put? Or, perhaps more importantly, what not to put?

Not everyone will have enough spare time to indulge in any hobbies. Between the demands of modern working life and children to look after, many people's idea of a hobby is having five minutes spare to watch 'Coronation Street'!

Popular activities they may be, but you should definitely look to exclude certain items that are guaranteed not to impress a prospective employer:

> Socialising (consistently voted No. 1 most common entry in this section)

> Watching TV/going shopping (undoubtedly the most uninteresting!)

> Listening to music (very common and hardly sounds very interesting)

> Clubbing

> Travel.

As always, there are exceptions. If you're looking to work in the travel sector then you should definitely make mention of your interest in travelling – and if you're planning to work in a night club then it's clearly alright to state your passion for clubbing. But in the vast majority of cases you should leave these out.

Relevancy

In an ideal world your interests (or at least one or two of them) would be relevant in some way to your job. If you are engaged in an activity which could be considered to have a connection with your work then you should certainly make a feature of this. Membership of relevant, amateur societies and clubs is always a bonus. Any team activities are of course likely to be relevant to almost any job.

Be specific

It is a good idea to try to 'qualify' your interests. For example, just saying 'Cooking' isn't going to be particularly interesting to the reader but 'Cooking (French and Italian)' is immediately much more memorable.

Positions of responsibility

It's always a good idea if you can subtly slip in mention of any positions of responsibility you hold outside of work. If your passion is, for example, football, and you're also the Captain of the local team, then do say so on your CV:

Football (Captain of local team)

Besides the obvious selling point of football being a team activity (and hence your being a 'team player'), you've immediately communicated your leadership qualities, your ability to take responsibility for others, your ability to commit yourself to a project, etc.

Personal achievements

As well as flagging up your professional achievements on your CV, don't be modest when it comes to your personal achievements. Personal achievements demonstrate talent and commitment just as much as, if not more so than, professional achievements. Imagine you've won the Celeste Art Prize for your oil paintings – or perhaps you've excelled at some particular sport. However, as with everything else on your CV, try to keep the focus on recent history. There's very little point in going too far back – the older the information, the weaker its impact.

Voluntary work

If you're actively involved in any voluntary work, for example for a charity, then *Interests and Activities* is the ideal place to make mention of this. Clearly this sort of activity should count in your favour with many employers. Not only does it show that you are civil-minded but it also indicates that you most likely have strong people skills. Don't be afraid to blow your own trumpet. However, do keep it short and to-the-point.

Unusual hobbies

Mainstream interests, for example horse riding, have the advantage that you're more likely to stumble upon a recruiter who shares the same interest. Conversely, it is probably unlikely that anyone reading your CV will share your interest in lizard breeding; however, that's not to say you wouldn't be invited for an interview anyway just to get a closer look at you! So there may be some advantage to displaying some originality in this section – but it's a lottery really and there's no firm advice I can give other than to avoid mentioning any interests which may cause offence among certain readers, for example hunting.

Don't go over the top

Whatever you do include, you should of course be able to back it up. If you mention chess to give your CV some intellectual clout but haven't actually played since you were at school then you could well come a cropper in your interview if your interviewer turns out to be a chess fan and asks you which openings to the game you favour!

BLOOPER!

Putting 'golf' on your CV to impress a corporate recruiter when you have in fact only been on a golf course twice in your entire life could be something that you come to regret in the future when your new manager is looking to organise a golfing weekend.

Order

You should give some thought to the order in which you list your *Interests and Activities*. Try to group them logically, e.g. instead of 'Football, Film/Cinema, Tennis and Creative Writing' – try 'Football, Tennis, Film/Cinema and Creative Writing', i.e. keep sports together and outdoor activities together and indoor or more cerebral activities together. It will read better that way.

Humour

Finally, I would firmly caution against humour. You might think it shows a sense of humour to say you enjoy 'Going out with mates every single night'. But the reader probably won't find this particularly funny.

BLOOPER!

I once saw a CV where the gentleman in question had, under *Interests and Activities*, simply written: 'Women'. Some recruiters might possibly find that funny. But the majority probably won't or, even if they do, certainly won't risk short-listing such a candidate.

CASE STUDY

Jane has a wide range of activities outside of work and, because she's got enough space available, she details her *Interests and Activities* in a separate section. And she rounds off her CV with a simple statement about her references.

Interests and Activities

Currently include: Badminton, Squash and Pilates
Theatre (local 'amateur dramatics') and Cinema (especially classic films)

Summary

> Just so long as the majority of recruiters and employers remain in favour of them, I almost always advocate the inclusion of a *Professional Profile*, followed by an *Objective*.

> While a *Key Skills* section is progressively less popular these days, it remains essential for the 'functional' CV type.

> Avoid a dry and boring list of your duties and responsibilities. You're not writing a job description; you're writing a compelling sales pitch.

> If you can include an *Achievements* section, then it can really make an instant and dramatic difference to the power of your CV.

> On balance, I remain firmly convinced that you most certainly should include an *Interests and Activities* section on your CV.

PART 3

THE 15 MOST COMMON CV WRITING MISTAKES – AND HOW TO AVOID THEM!

I have seen many thousands of CVs, covering pretty much every possible kind of job, and the difference in them is vast. However, the same common mistakes crop up time and time again. Too many jobseekers miss out on their dream job because of a small number of easily avoided blunders.

Some of the mistakes that people make when writing a CV are very obvious and others are much more subtle. The CV Centre has conducted a comprehensive analysis of over 2,500 CVs to derive a 'top 15'. In this chapter, I will list these 15 most common CV writing mistakes and refer you back to previous chapters where necessary, both to explain why they are a mistake – and also to explain how to avoid them.

1 Inclusion of photographs

People often include photos of themselves on their CV. Don't! Unless you are applying to be a model or wish to work as an actor/actress, then including a photo with/on your CV is definitely not recommended – at least not within the UK.

The whole point of a CV is that the recruiter has a brief, factual description of your abilities, and photographs often allow recruiters, rightly or wrongly, to develop a preconceived idea of you as a person. And this might well count against you. They may have an irrational aversion to facial hair for example! An interview is the most appropriate place for the recruiter to first see an applicant, not the CV.

For a longer discussion on the topic of photos, please refer to Chapter 1, 'Aesthetics and presentation: looking good on paper'.

2 Inappropriate heading

Your CV should be headed with your name – and just your name – boldly and clearly – before any other details – contact details, etc. It should not be headed 'Curriculum Vitae' or 'CV' or anything else.

Just your name. And only your first name and your last name.

It is true that, traditionally, CVs were headed with 'Curriculum Vitae', or suchlike, but this convention is very much on the way out now – which is probably a good thing, given how frequently it is misspelled!

BLOOPER!

One candidate actually headed his CV, 'Kuriculam Vitay'!

For further details on how to head your CV, please refer to Chapter 4, 'Personal details'.

3 Missing or inappropriate email addresses

Whilst having no email address at all on your CV is clearly a problem, it's not something I see very often. Far more common is the use of fun or jokey email addresses.

Whilst these may be fine for corresponding with friends and family, employers will probably regard more 'serious' email addresses as simply more professional.

BLOOPER!

··

You might have the perfect CV, but if your email address is mrluvverman@example.com then it may harm your chances!

I would suggest you open a new email account to use for professional purposes (e.g. Hotmail or Yahoo) and keep your professional correspondence separate from your personal correspondence.

To learn more about how to handle email addresses, please refer to Chapter 4, 'Personal details'.

4 Superfluous personal details at the top of the CV

My clients often feel that it is compulsory to include details such as their marital status, nationality, number (and ages) of children/dependants, etc. While, yes, it certainly used to be the norm to include this sort of information on a CV, it is now increasingly rare, given modern anti-discrimination legislation, to find these sorts of details on a CV. They simply aren't relevant.

Too many candidates get too personal. A recruiter does not need to know whether or not you're married, how many children you have, where you like to go on holiday, what your partner's name is, what you normally have for breakfast ... These facts should not affect whether or not you can do the job! They simply clutter up your CV, making it harder for recruiters to get to the key information that they really need to see.

I talk about this subject in greater detail in Chapter 4, 'Personal details'.

5 Lack of clear section headings/separation of sections

It is vitally important for your CV to be easy for the reader to scan quickly and, to this end, clear section headings and separation of sections are essential. I often recommend the use of lines or other graphic devices in this respect, although there are other ways of achieving a clearer separation.

Issues such as white space, readability and graphics are covered in detail in Chapter 1, 'Aesthetics and presentation: looking good on paper'.

6 Writing in the first person

The words 'I' and 'me' are often used repeatedly in homemade CVs. CVs should be written exclusively in the third person. Making a CV too personal by using 'I' and 'me' tends to look unprofessional. It can convey an impression of arrogance and egocentrism: 'I this …', 'I that …', 'I the other …', 'me, me, me!' But most of all it's just too informal. It might seem unnatural to write a document about yourself and yet never use either 'I' or 'me', but recruitment experts conclusively agree that this is the best way to do it. Don't give your reader I-strain!

The third person can sound a little stuffy at times but it generally reads better and comes across as more professional. It gives you greater scope to brag about yourself without actually sounding as if you're bragging!

How do you write something in the third person? Take a look at Chapter 2, 'Content and style: what to say and how to say it'.

7 Lack of proper Professional Profile and/or Objective

A *Professional Profile* is a brief statement at the very beginning of a CV which, in the space of a few short lines, conveys to readers an overall impression of your key personal and professional characteristics. It's essentially an introduction and should give readers an overview before they read on in further detail.

An *Objective* section explains your preferred career direction and details what you hope to achieve from your future career.

It is very important to include a sufficiently detailed and very carefully phrased *Professional Profile* and, if space permits, *Objective* at the beginning of the CV. The reader needs to know instantly what you're about and what sort of position you are looking for. This is also a key area to consider tailoring for different applications. It's one of the first (and sometimes only) sections the reader will see and consequently gives you a vital opportunity to make a powerful first impression on them.

I tell you how to go about constructing these sections in Chapter 5, 'Professional profile' and Chapter 6, 'Objective'.

8 Inappropriate section order

It's extremely important to choose an appropriate order for the various sections of your CV. For example, the decision whether to put your *Education and Qualifications* before or after your *Career History* is critical.

It all depends on what is your greater selling point. You should make sure that all your most important information is conveyed on the first page or, for a one-page CV, in the top half of the page.

Which do you feel is most likely to be of interest to a prospective employer? Your *Education and Qualifications* or your *Career History*?

I help you to answer this question in Chapter 3, 'Structure: which type of CV is right for you?'

9 No bullet pointing

In today's fast-paced world, recruiters no longer have the time to read large, solid blocks of prose. They need to extract the information they need – and they need to do it fast. Long paragraphs of prose are tiresome for a recruiter to read right through and, as a result, many simply won't bother.

And this is where bullet-pointing comes in, although, unfortunately, so many people fail to use it to their advantage within their CV. Whilst I wouldn't recommend you use bullet-pointing everywhere – and I would actually recommend against it for your *Professional Profile* – I would very strongly recommend its use in your *Career History*.

I talk more about bullet-pointing and the importance of readability in Chapter 1, 'Aesthetics and presentation: looking good on paper'.

10 Reverse chronological order not used

It is a standard convention on CVs to use reverse chronological order, i.e. to present your most recent information first, followed by older – and consequently less relevant – information. And I would strongly suggest you make sure your CV conforms to this.

Many people find this illogical and don't feel comfortable with the idea. But look at it this way:

Should the first job you ever did – for example, working in a pub to support your studies – really be the first thing a prospective employer sees when looking at your *Career History*? If you're now a Managing Director, it's going to look a tad irrelevant. And when they look at your *Education and Qualifications*, what should they read first? Details of the GCSEs you sat ten years ago? Or details of the MA in Applied Communication that you've just completed?

More about this in Chapter 3, 'Structure: which type of CV is right for you?'

11 Excessive details of interests

You should aim to keep your interests section brief. As with every other aspect of your CV, do include what you feel will count in your favour – but be selective about it. Many people write far too much in this section.

No 'Socialising' or 'Clubbing' please, as a recruiter will inevitably imagine you are going to come into work hungover on a regular basis! Even if you do plan to go into work hungover on a regular basis, it's best not to advertise the fact! And best not to risk putting down 'Travel' either (unless you want to work in the travel sector), as a potential employer will inevitably worry that you are about to take a long career break to see the world.

BLOOPER!

Choose carefully. You may indeed have a passion for model railways – but do you really want the recruiter to know that?

The *Interests and Activities* section of your CV is discussed in much greater detail in Chapter 12, 'Interests and activities'.

12 Date of birth included

I often get asked whether or not you should include your date of birth (or age) on a CV. The old answer to this used to be that you should include it, because recruiters expect to see it and so if you don't include it then it'll just draw attention to the fact.

However, this advice has now changed – since the introduction of the Employment Equality (Age) Regulations 2006. And, besides, any recruiter worth his or her salt will be able to deduce pretty accurately exactly how old you are just by looking at your education, qualifications and experience.

There is also a security (identity fraud) risk involved in volunteering this sort of highly personal data to all and sundry. Should your CV fall into the wrong hands, this is precisely the sort of information an identity fraudster needs to clone your identity.

13 Referees included

Details of referees generally shouldn't be included on your CV. They're a waste of valuable space! They clutter it up and, more importantly, you will find that your referees get pestered unnecessarily by time wasters. By the time they have handled their umpteenth enquiry of the day, they are a lot less likely to say nice things about you!

A simple statement at the bottom of your CV saying, 'References are available on request' is more than sufficient because it's not information that a recruiter needs to have up front. When your application progresses to the next level and there is serious talk of a job offer then that is the time to provide these details.

There are of course exceptions to the rule – and I talk at greater length about the topic of referees in Chapter 11, 'Other details'.

14 Spelling, grammar and typos

STATISTIC

Our research has shown that 60 per cent of the CVs we receive contain linguistic errors.

It is impossible to stress enough how important this issue is. Spelling and grammatical errors are among the most irritating errors a recruiter sees, among the most damaging errors you can make – and are also among the most easily avoided. The answer is to check, check and check again – and then have someone else check for good measure!

Just one misplaced letter can make a huge difference to your career prospects. Common errors include candidates stating, for example, that they 'worked closely with the Finance Manger'.

BLOOPER!

In one unfortunate case, the individual in question got very confused about the difference between 'role' and 'roll'. He kept referring throughout both his CV and his cover letter to the various 'rolls' he had had, e.g. 'an important roll in the finance department', 'sharing a roll with another colleague', etc.

For the full story on spelling, grammar and typos please refer to Chapter 2, 'Content and style: what to say and how to say it'.

15 Length

This is one of the most common problems I see when people prepare their own CVs – they're quite simply too long.

I have seen CVs over 30 pages long (true!) with photocopies of all their certificates on top of that.

This is not an autobiography you're writing. It's a curriculum vitae. It's a lot shorter!

I always advocate a one-page CV if it is feasible – and some recruitment agencies, especially head-hunters, may insist on a one-page CV.

Failing that, two pages are entirely acceptable and, in certain circumstances, it may be acceptable for a CV to run to three or more pages, but only for some senior or very technical posts, e.g. medical, engineering, etc.

For a longer discussion about the length of your CV see Chapter 3, 'Structure: which type of CV is right for you?'

For more information on those 'special cases' please see Chapter 14, 'Special cases – professions where the rules are different'.

16 Lack of achievements section

Yes, I know I said this chapter would cover the 15 most common CV writing mistakes but everyone loves a bonus don't they?

So here's a 16th mistake for you: failing to include an *Achievements* section.

Including an *Achievements* section will not necessarily be appropriate for everyone but if it could be deemed to be appropriate to your circumstances then I do feel it would be a mistake to leave it out.

Please refer to Chapter 10, 'Achievements', to learn all about the *Achievements* section.

PART 4

WHEN THE USUAL RULES DON'T APPLY...

Chapter **13**

Ten solutions for ten potential problems

Everybody is different and every CV is consequently different. Some people's lives and career paths are relatively simple; others are much more complex.

In this chapter I will tackle how to deal with ten common and potentially tricky situations in the most positive way possible:

1 What if I have little or no relevant work experience?

2 What if my current job isn't relevant to the job I am now looking for?

3 What if there are gaps in my *Career History*?

4 What if I have changed jobs far more frequently than the average?

5 What if I've been with the same organisation for my entire career?

6 What if I am overqualified for the role for which I am applying?

7 What if I am under-qualified for the role for which I am applying?

8 What if I have been dismissed from a previous position?

9 What if I've been made redundant?

10 What if I am worried that my age may count against me?

1 What if I have little or no relevant work experience?

The most common reason for a candidate to lack experience is that they're newly qualified – possibly a recent school leaver or a recent graduate. The answer is to make the most of what you've got.

Clearly you need to lead with your *Education and Qualifications* section. This is going to be your biggest selling point. It should be the most significant feature of your CV – and you should give it all the attention it deserves.

Following this, you should pick out skills you've acquired during your studies at school or university – regardless of whether or not you've yet had a chance to apply them in the workplace – and feature them as bullet points within a *Key Skills* section. This should come immediately after your *Education and Qualifications*.

Even if your work experience has been intermittent, part-time and principally for the purposes of helping to fund your studies rather than having any relevance to your future career, you should still find it worth mentioning. Some workplace experience is always better than none.

You are also entitled to expand the *Interests and Activities* section to include, for example, roles of responsibility you held in societies or clubs, volunteer work, etc. Normally this is a section you should keep brief – but recent school leavers and graduates are entitled to pad it out just a little bit.

Don't worry if your CV is only one page long; if you have little or no work experience then a recruiter won't be expecting a two-page CV from you.

Of course, another reason for lacking relevant experience is that you have quite simply decided you wish to change career path.

2 What if my current job isn't relevant to the job I am now looking for?

If you're trying to change career path then this will be one occasion where you might very well be better served by a functional CV.

First of all you need to declare your future career intentions in an appropriately phrased *Objective*. This will help to avoid any confusion on the part of the reader.

Your previous experience might not be directly relevant but you should still present it in the best possible light. Try to focus on the transferable skills and abilities that you have developed by making use of a *Key Skills* section.

You can also dilute any attention which might be focused on your current role by following your *Key Skills* section with a *Key Experience* section. The *Key Experience* section should highlight aspects of your *Career History* that are most relevant to the role you are now looking to undertake.

Your circumstances may be such that you are keen to apply for work in an industry or sector in which you used to work but have departed from in your recent employment history. For example, you could be applying for a job in banking which you used to work in a few years back but your more recent experience is in retail.

In this sort of situation I would recommend you contemplate separating out the different types of experience, for example instead of one section of *Key Experience* you could have a section on *Banking Experience* followed by one on *Retail Experience*.

3 What if there are gaps in my Career History?

Unexplained gaps in your employment record can naturally raise concerns in the minds of recruiters. They may think you have something to hide! And many recruiters will immediately draw their own conclusions (generally not very positive ones) and reject your application.

A useful 'trick' I have already mentioned is to cover up brief chronological gaps by only listing years, not months within your *Career History*. I'd recommend doing this regardless of whether or not you have any gaps. I consider listing all the months to be unnecessary detail (although some recruiters, especially some recruitment agencies, may still insist on all the months being listed – and medical professionals should always provide full details).

If you have larger gaps than can be concealed by simply omitting the months, then that can be problematic – but there are of course solutions. Most people have a gap or two in their career history. It's very common and not normally anything to worry about.

How you go about handling a gap depends on the reasons for that gap.

Naturally, if you have a gap as a result of voluntary work, self-employment, freelance work, etc. then it's not really a gap at all and you should see this all as part and parcel of your *Career History*.

However, there are many other reasons for gaps within your career history – but only one that an employer is really going to view favourably:

> further training/education

Other common – and conceivably constructive – reasons include:

> raising a child
> caring for another dependant
> travel.

But there are also reasons which will definitely be viewed negatively:

> inability to find a suitable position
> ill health
> imprisonment.

If the reason for the gap in your career history isn't obviously negative, then there shouldn't be a gap in your CV – you should include a brief entry explaining the situation.

Further training/education: this is very simple and doesn't really qualify as a gap at all. Provided you clearly state the dates in both your *Career History* and *Education and Qualifications* sections the reader will hopefully be intelligent enough to put two and two together.

Raising a child/caring for another dependant: if you took time out of your career in order to raise a child – or care for another dependant – then it is very much your own private affair. However, it's definitely best to include a brief entry on your CV explaining the circumstances rather than leaving an unexplained gap.

Travel: taking a sabbatical to go travelling is often (but not always!) seen by an employer as a positive thing. Many will believe that the cultural awareness and sense of independence you will have gained as a result of the experience will prove to be of value to them. Also, if you've already taken time out to travel then it means you're less likely to suddenly disappear to travel the world just as they've got you settled in. (This is a common worry among employers, particularly when it comes to younger employees.) Include a brief explanation on your CV (and I do mean brief), making reference to any temporary and part-time work you might have undertaken in other countries, if that could be an additional selling point for you.

Unfortunately, general employment and ill health are unlikely – at least initially – to be viewed favourably by a recruiter. And imprisonment certainly won't be viewed favourably.

My considered advice for dealing with these cases is to avoid making an issue of them on your CV. Research shows that less than half of recruiters notice gaps during their initial sift anyway. Rather than try to explain yourself within your CV – thus drawing attention to the issue – you'd be much better off covering such matters at interview. With a bit of luck, the recruiter won't even notice at interview either!

4 What if I have changed jobs far more frequently than the average?

Getting through a large number of jobs in a short period of time can ring alarm bells in recruiters' heads. They may conclude that you are not capable of committing yourself or of maintaining your focus. They may deem you to be fickle. It's a natural enough assumption – even if it's not justified.

BLOOPER!

As one candidate stated on his CV:

Note: please don't misconstrue my 13 different jobs as job-hopping. I have never quit a job.

There may be any number of reasons why you have changed jobs so frequently. Explaining the reasons isn't important; the key is to emphasise what you have learned and what you are now able to offer an employer as a result of this breadth of experience. Highlight the diversity of the organisations you worked for and, therefore, the variety of skills which you acquired as a result.

And the best way to communicate this is to use the functional type of CV.

Implement a *Key Skills* section highlighting the transferable skills you have developed during the course of your career – administrative, organisational, interpersonal, etc. skills.

You should then proceed to a *Key Experience* section, citing specific examples to support what you have said in the *Key Skills* section.

And you should conclude with a *Career Summary* rather than a full *Career History*.

How do you know what to put in and what to leave out if you've had lots of work experience?

As always, include information that's in your favour and leave out information that isn't.

And finally, if you're applying for a permanent role, make it perfectly clear that you are indeed now looking for a permanent role – even if you aren't actually planning to stay for long!

5 What if I've been with the same organisation for my entire career?

There are both positive and negative ways in which a recruiter will view candidates who have worked for the same organisation for all – or the majority – of their career. Whilst some people may consider this to be a reflection of commitment and loyalty, others may see it as a sign that they are not keen on change – or have, for whatever reason, been unable to change.

On balance, I don't feel this to be nearly as much of a problem as some candidates believe it to be. You'd be surprised how many top executives have forged almost all of their careers in just one single organisation. Staying with one employer did, in fact, used to be entirely normal – and desirable. It's only in recent decades that people's career paths have become so much more complicated.

A career is a career – whether you've worked for only one organisation or a dozen. You will no doubt possess a wealth of transferable skills, abilities and experience, and you should make sure your CV communicates this comprehensively. During the course of your career you will most likely have undertaken a variety of roles and each of these should be given the attention they deserve.

TOP TIP

You must of course be prepared for an interviewer to ask you why you've stayed so long with one, single employer – but you shouldn't fear that this fact alone will hold you back in any way.

6 What if I am overqualified for the role for which I am applying?

This is not a common situation – but one that certainly does arise, especially in times of higher than average unemployment. Alternatively, you may have decided to take a step back from your career for personal reasons – for example to achieve a better work–life balance.

Being overqualified for a position is a significant hurdle, as employing such an individual can pose a major risk to an employer. Are you desperate and prepared to take any job going whether you are really interested in it or not? Are you going to be disappointed with the role and move on quickly? Are you going to cause problems in the hierarchy?

You clearly don't want recruiters to be asking themselves these sorts of questions.

The usual rule with CV writing is of course, 'If you've got it, flaunt it!' However, in this situation, the secret is to downplay your qualifications. Make them less prominent.

If you're overqualified by virtue of your actual academic qualifications then you should make sure that you place your *Career History* before your *Education and Qualifications* – moving this discreetly to a second page if possible.

If, on the other hand, you could be seen as being overqualified as a result of your current or most recent employment then, while you should of course adhere to the rule of highlighting skills and experience which are most relevant to the job for which you are applying, you should selectively tone down the scale of your duties and responsibilities.

It's all a matter of getting the pitch right. You're pitching for a particular job so make sure that your CV reflects this – and doesn't give the impression that you'd rather be doing a different job. If you fail to convince the reader that you really want this job then you clearly don't stand a chance.

7 What if I am under-qualified for the role for which I am applying?

Being under-qualified for a role is a very different case from being overqualified.

I'm afraid there is really very little point applying for a job if you simply do not have the required qualifications and experience – it's a waste of your own time and the employer's time. For example, if a job advert specifies that the candidate must be highly proficient with MS Access and you only have a basic working knowledge, then there is probably very little point in your applying for the position. You can be absolutely sure that there will be applicants who do fully meet the criteria and you clearly can't compete with them. It's a very competitive job market out there.

However, there are of course exceptions …

If you only just fall short of the criteria but feel you have other qualities which will give you an edge, then it may still be worth a shot. It's very much a matter of judgement whether or not you should proceed with your application.

CASE STUDY

The advert for the job Jane is applying for stipulates they require:

... a thorough working knowledge of MS Access.

Although Jane has little practical experience it its application, she has recently completed a CLAIT qualification and so does have a very good theoretical knowledge. Demonstrating a strong theoretical understanding of a selection criterion, even if you have not yet had the opportunity in practice, is an allowable exception to our normal rule.

To give you another example, a job advert might state that the employer is looking for someone with a minimum of five years' experience and you only have four – but you have an additional and relevant qualification which is not mentioned in the advert. Look at it from the recruiter's point of view. What is more important to them – the extra year's experience or the additional qualification?

Whilst you should always make the very most of what you've got, unless you have a 'hidden ace' up your sleeve, in terms of your qualifications and experience, you should avoid applying for jobs where you don't comfortably match their criteria.

8 What if I have been dismissed from a previous position?

What if you were sacked for gross misconduct from your previous position (or any position, for that matter)?

I made the point in Chapter 8, 'Career history' that you shouldn't take up valuable room on your CV explaining your reasons for leaving – whether you were dismissed or left of your own accord. That space can be better spent incorporating additional sales points.

You know by now that it is not advisable to include anything in your CV that does not add value or could appear in any way negative. And being sacked for gross misconduct obviously meets that definition!

Whilst you shouldn't make any mention of this on your CV, you may still find yourself having to explain the situation at interview. I have two pieces of advice for you on how to handle this:

> ➤ You must be truthful; it's all too easy for a prospective employer to check these sorts of detail.

➤ Convey the circumstances as calmly and dispassionately as possible, acknowledge responsibility for the causes of your dismissal and, above all else, convince the interviewer that you learned a great deal from the experience and that this will never, ever happen again.

BLOOPER!

··

The company made me a scapegoat, just like my three previous employers.

---

9 What if I've been made redundant?

I fully appreciate that redundancy is a difficult time and that there's often little justice in an employer's choice of who to make redundant. I empathise entirely. However, while it's unlikely that you've been made redundant through any fault of your own, the fact that you have been made redundant may unfortunately be perceived in a negative fashion by a prospective employer.

The simplest solution to this is to not make any mention of the fact on your CV. I've already explained that including your reasons for leaving a job is unnecessary – and redundancy is definitely no exception.

The subject may of course come up in interview. However, you must conceal any bitterness and resentment you may feel and instead convey to the interviewer that 'such is life', 'these things happen', it wasn't your fault. It is the position that is redundant, not the individual person. Under no circumstances should you criticise the employer that laid you off. Rather than dwell on negative aspects, you must aim to emphasise any positive outcomes – for example that it gave you the opportunity to undertake some valuable training.

10 What if I am worried that my age may count against me?

Clearly, your age should not count against you. Various pieces of legislation, notably the Employment Equality (Age) Regulations 2006, are designed to prevent this. However, we all know the reality is that discrimination persists regardless of such legislation and the last thing you want is for your age to be a stumbling block when it comes to getting yourself an interview.

Too many candidates 'over a certain age' see their age as a negative aspect of their CV. Before you even start writing your CV, get this kind of thinking right out of your head. Concentrate on the wealth of experience you have to offer. You've spent a lifetime learning and developing your skills. There's absolutely no justification for someone counting your age against you. William Gladstone was still going strong as British Prime Minister at the age of 84!

Having got yourself into a more positive frame of mind, let's look at a few practical measures you can take to help counter any possible discrimination.

The best technique at your disposal is to place the focus very firmly on your most recent history and to radically summarise earlier information. I would suggest splitting your *Career History* into a *Recent Career History* section spanning the past decade or so and a *Previous Employment* section. The former can go into appropriate detail but the latter should only list job titles, employers' names and locations – no dates or details of duties, responsibilities and achievements.

Your *Career History* will almost inevitably be more important than your *Education and Qualifications* and should therefore be listed before your *Education and Qualifications*, certainly not after. If your most recent qualifications go back several decades then there's absolutely no need to include the dates within this section. And if your qualifications are limited to 0-levels passed in the 1960s, then why mention them at all? They have absolutely no relevance to your current employability.

While an *Achievements* section is almost always a welcome addition to a CV, make sure you limit your entries to recent achievements. Don't go back any further than the jobs you've included in your *Recent Career History*.

By making it hard to guess your age from your CV, you may arouse some curiosity – but it shouldn't reduce your chances of being called for an interview. On the contrary, it has been shown to increase your chances.

Chapter **14**

Special cases –
professions where
the rules are
different

Certain professions and lines of work have specific requirements when it comes to CV writing. Whilst a lot of the advice I give you in *The CV Book* is generic and can be applied to anybody, regardless of their profession, in this chapter I will cover the particular requirements of a number of professions where the rules are somewhat different.

Medical CVs

Although recruitment to medical posts is increasingly conducted via application forms, CVs are still essential for many vacancies.

As a medical professional, you'll possess extensive qualifications following many years of training – and very possibly many years' experience. Your prospective employers will definitely want to know all about this and a medical CV will, therefore, inevitably be more complex – and longer – than the average CV.

You may possess quite an extensive variety of professional experience, including numerous posts you only held for a short period. As such, your *Career History* should state not only years but precise months. You may even decide a functional CV would suit you best.

Besides the 'standard' CV sections I have covered so far in this book, there are a number of other possible sections which can be appropriate for a medical CV:

> Clinical Skills

> Audits

> Research

> Presentations

> Publications

> Teaching.

TOP TIP

You should aim to order the sections of your CV logically and more or less according to the value they contribute.

As well as providing comprehensive details of your *Education and Qualifications*, it is also important to demonstrate CPD. Yours is a profession where you are expected to be continually learning – and much value is placed on this by employers.

Whilst you shouldn't generally include details of referees on a CV, medical CVs are an exception. The reader will be expecting full details of your referees right from the start.

You will also be expected to provide details of your professional registration, including reference numbers. These can be listed under *Other Details*. But don't include details of your hepatitis B status; it's jumping the gun.

Fitting all this into two pages is a fairly tall order and so it's absolutely fine for your finished CV to run to three, four or even five pages. However, if it starts to exceed five pages then you may be falling into the trap of packing in an excessive amount of information – and this could make it harder for your key selling points to stand out.

For example, while it's certainly a good idea to list any research projects, it would be a mistake to provide too much detail. Try to summarise and remain concise. Prospective employers can always ask for further information if they require it – maybe at your interview.

Finally, you should of course adopt an appropriate tone or 'voice' – a formal, academic style will work best.

Academic and scientific CVs

Academic and scientific CVs have many similarities with medical CVs.

There will be a lot of information that you need to communicate – and that a prospective employer will be expecting you to communicate. However, you must be careful not to provide too much detail – overly long descriptions of projects, excessive technical detail, etc.

You might be itching to write extensive descriptions of the work you've undertaken but it's vital to summarise and stick to the main points. You can always elaborate at your interview if necessary – but packing in too much information into your CV is likely to reduce your chances of winning an interview in the first place.

It could be appropriate to implement additional sections detailing any publications, etc. However, the general recommendation for academic and scientific CVs is that they should not exceed two pages – three as an absolute maximum. You really do have to be concise.

You may need to use specialist terminology to illustrate your points but, as I have previously pointed out, excessive jargon is not a good idea. If you need to use a specialist/technical term that you are not sure the reader will understand then it is perfectly acceptable to follow it with a brief definition in brackets.

Teaching CVs

As with most CVs, the way you approach writing a teaching CV will depend on the level you've reached in your career. NQTs (newly qualified teachers) will focus on their qualifications, whereas more senior teachers will focus on their practical experience.

Teaching CVs do have a tendency to be longer than the average CV – but you should still be aiming for two pages maximum if possible. For a start, you'll normally be backing up your CV with a fairly lengthy cover letter. (Cover letters are particularly important for job applications within the teaching profession.)

TOP TIP

CPD is essential within teaching and should be a prominent feature of your CV – preferably in a separate, dedicated section. You could include details of any INSET (in-service education and training) days.

IT skills should be highlighted. They are, of course, increasingly important, especially with interactive learning resources, etc. now being commonplace.

Extracurricular activities are also of particular interest within teaching. Recruiters will be looking for evidence that you really want to get involved with all aspects of school life, contribute to the community and build relationships with their students both in and out of the classroom.

Legal CVs

Legal CVs don't differ greatly from 'normal' CVs. You still need to keep to a two-page maximum and you still need to ensure your 'sales pitch' is as strong as it can be. However, there are a couple of differences you need to be aware of.

The sheer competitiveness of the sector means that recruiters may want to look at your academic background in great detail. As such, a legal CV should be very comprehensive in this respect, including full details of institutions attended, grades achieved, etc. at all levels of study.

You should also be very precise when detailing your *Career History*, citing cases of particular importance, significant court results, etc. But don't get too bogged down in detail; stick to the key points.

One final word of warning: You should of course be especially careful not to disclose any information which is legally or commercially sensitive.

IT CVs

IT CVs are frequently very complex and, while there's a lot of information you need to communicate, it's vital to focus on communicating that information clearly and concisely – being especially careful in your use of jargon.

You may have worked on a wide range of different projects and contracts and consequently find that the functional type of CV is most appropriate.

Highlight your specific technical skills in a separate section of your CV, broken down by category, for example:

> Hardware
> Software
> Programming Languages
> Network Protocols.

You should also flag up any relevant affiliations such as membership of the British Computer Society or accreditation with Microsoft, Cisco, etc.

While the goal is a two-page CV, if you have a broad range of experience and a high degree of technical proficiency then it is acceptable for your CV to run to three pages. But don't use this additional space to pad out your CV with unnecessary detail.

Engineering CVs

The rules for engineering CVs are very similar to those for IT CVs:

> The functional type of CV may be the most appropriate.
> You can break down your skills under separate section headings.
> Affiliations, memberships and accreditation should be highlighted.
> It's acceptable for your CV to run to three pages if necessary.

Architecture and design CVs

If you work within a highly creative and artistic field then a lot of the standard rules of CV design can be thrown out of the window!

Prospective employers will be on the lookout for original thinkers – and this will impact on the way you design your CV. They'll be looking for you to demonstrate a bit of flair.

The content of your CV won't be drastically different from the average CV, but the way it is presented could be distinctly different.

I won't be giving any precise design tips – it's your field of expertise. Let your imagination run riot! However, I would warn you not to lose sight of the importance of readability.

Performing arts CVs

As a performer, you'll probably be well aware that the CV you need bears little resemblance to a traditional CV.

Issues such as your age (or playing range), height, hair colour, eye colour, ethnicity and frame/build – which would never normally appear on a CV – suddenly take centre stage.

You should also focus the spotlight on that all-important Equity Number.

Subsequent sections of your CV could cover your TV, film, theatre, voice-over, etc. credits, as well as special skills such as singing, playing the flute, scuba diving, skiing, juggling, languages spoken, accents mastered, etc. You may even wish to include your agent's contact details. But try to keep the finished CV down to one single page.

You'll also need to arrange for a winning headshot – choose your photographer carefully if you don't want to bring down the curtain on your career – and you may even decide to print your CV onto the back of your headshot, rather than onto a normal sheet of paper.

You've chosen to work in a very challenging sector and, as with any other sector, a powerful CV can really help you to upstage the competition.

Break a leg!

Military/civilian transition CVs

A career in the Armed Services is clearly unlike any other. However, for most service personnel a time will come when they wish to return to Civvy Street.

It's a very big change.

However, you need to remember just how much you have to offer a prospective employer – discipline, courage, motivation, leadership and coaching skills, etc. While you might not have much in the way of directly relevant experience, you possess a plethora of highly valued transferable skills – skills which many employers are actively searching for.

The key to successfully writing a military/civilian transition CV is to take off your military cap and start thinking from the point of view of your prospective employers. There's much you will have to say about your military career but try to communicate in terms that a civilian will understand.

It's an excellent idea to include details of awards, honours, volunteer activities, etc. but endeavour to keep your readers in mind at all times. What is it that they're really looking for?

A functional CV, firmly focusing on your skills and abilities, is undoubtedly the way to go.

Chapter **15**

CVs and résumés – looking for work abroad

Fashions and accepted norms for CV writing can vary quite considerably from country to country. In many countries a CV isn't even called a CV; it could be called a résumé or any one of a number of local terms.

In *The CV Book* my focus is very much on the UK. However, in this chapter I will briefly discuss the particular requirements of a small selection of different countries. These are all countries I know to be popular among our clients when it comes to living and working abroad.

Whilst most of the basic principles remain the same, there are certainly many subtle – but important – differences.

Ireland (Éire)

Irish CVs have traditionally been much longer than UK CVs. However, this is steadily changing with more and more employers preferring the standard maximum of two pages.

Being a bilingual country, language skills are of above average interest to Irish employers. Make sure that you detail the languages you speak in full – including the level (and specifying which is your mother tongue).

The *Interests and Activities* section is particularly popular in Ireland; you are consequently entitled to elaborate on this section more so than you would do in the UK.

A final key difference is the way you handle referees. You can list on a separate sheet the details of at least two referees – either one professional and one personal or perhaps both your current and previous employers. Stating 'References are available on request' is permissible nonetheless; again, more and more employers are adapting to the UK style of doing things.

France and Belgium

First of all, the French use exactly the same term 'CV' that we use in the UK. They don't say, *'un résumé'* (at least not in this context).

French CVs tend to include a lot of detail which we now consider superfluous in the UK. Date of birth (or age), nationality, marital status and details of children are all virtually compulsory for French CVs. There's no need to include details of referees though; you can simply state, 'Références disponibles sur demande'.

French CVs are, nevertheless, briefer than UK CVs – one-page CVs are a lot more common than in the UK, even for individuals with many years' experience. Two pages is an absolute maximum.

Whilst you shouldn't include a *Professional Profile*, the *Objective* section is particularly important in France – and they don't just want to know your current objectives; they'll be interested in your career objectives for the next five years.

Including a photograph is popular in France. Naturally, it is important to ensure that this is a high-quality photograph – while it should be passport-size, it should not be passport-quality! If you're serious about getting a job, I'd recommend you consider using a professional photographer rather than an automated booth.

You can attach the photograph to the front of your CV, for example using a paperclip. However, I feel it is more visually impressive to design your CV in such a way as to leave an appropriate space for the photograph (the top right-hand corner) and then carefully glue it in place. There's also a lot less chance this way of your photo getting separated and being lost. You should, however, write your name and contact details on the back of the photo – just in case.

One final bit of advice: always write your last name in BLOCK CAPITALS. It's just the way they do things in France.

TOP TIP

To foreign employers, your gender won't necessarily be easy to deduce from your first name. Help them out by stating clearly, in their own language, what your title is, for example in France 'Mrs' becomes 'Mme'.

Germany, Austria and Switzerland

A German CV isn't a CV or a résumé. It's a 'Lebenslauf' (all nouns are capitalised in German) and should always be of the chronological (reverse chronological) type, not the functional type.

Date of birth, place of birth and nationality are all required details. Marital status is popular but not obligatory.

A photograph is also generally required. You should follow the same guidelines as for France, above, in this respect.

Unless there's direct relevance to your work, don't include an *Interests and Activities* section.

Applying to work for a German organisation can be quite a bureaucratic process! You are likely to be required to provide photocopies of the following documents, if available:

> certificates for all formal qualifications gained

> certificates or diplomas for all further training undertaken

> work/residence permit

> driving licence.

It used to be accepted practice to bind all these documents together in a folder. However, a simple staple will now suffice if there aren't too many pages.

Whilst you may have to submit a lot of accompanying paperwork, the CV itself should be kept reasonably brief – two pages maximum – but it should still be very comprehensive, listing full details of all qualifications, including grades.

Italy

Comprehensive personal details are expected – date of birth, place of birth, nationality, marital status and details of children. However, as in German-speaking countries, unless there's direct relevance to your work you shouldn't include an *Interests and Activities* section.

Apart from that, styles vary widely – although I'd recommend you generally follow the UK format and keep your CV down to two pages maximum.

One interesting point is that Italy has very strict privacy laws and it is essential to grant the reader permission to make appropriate use of your CV. You should add the statement, 'Autorizzo l'utilizzo dei miei dati personali in conformità alla legge 675/96' to the bottom of your CV, meaning, 'I agree to disclose my personal information according to law 675/96'. This must be followed by your signature.

Spain

As in Italy, comprehensive personal details are expected – right down to your passport or ID card number. It is also very popular to include a photograph.

Unlike Italy, you can even include details of your *Interests and Activities*.

The United States of America

A CV is of course a 'résumé' in the USA.

The most important difference is the style. Your résumé should be written in a more aggressive style than a UK CV; you really have to sell yourself. The *Objective* section is critical; you need to pitch hard and fast. Try to think like an American!

The functional approach is also very popular, focusing on your key skills and experience – your key selling points. Details such as *Interests and Activities* are irrelevant.

Anti-discrimination legislation is just as stringent in the USA as it now is in the UK. You should therefore exclude all the same personal details you'd exclude in the UK – your date of birth, marital status, etc. You should also never include a photograph unless specifically asked to do so.

A résumé preferably only covers a single page, although two pages are acceptable.

And don't forget to use American spelling!

TOP TIP

If you're a European citizen and applying for work outside of the EU then it's important to highlight your right to work in the country in question.

Canada

Canada is a country of two languages – English and French. In the English-speaking regions you should adopt the American résumé style of CV. In the French-speaking regions, you should use the French CV style. However, it is worth noting that most Canadians use the term 'résumé' to describe the finished document, regardless of their mother tongue.

Australia and New Zealand

Down Under, they also prefer the term 'résumé'. However, Australian and New Zealand résumés are longer than American ones – typically two to three pages.

They follow broadly the same format as UK CVs except, being longer, you will be expected to be more comprehensive.

Details of referees are also commonly included and should be listed at the bottom of your second or third page. It is unlikely, however, to be held against you if you prefer to say, 'References are available on request'.

South Africa

The terms 'résumé' and 'CV' are used interchangeably in South Africa – but both have the same meaning.

While it is acceptable for your CV to run to several pages, I'd still recommend you aim to be concise and keep to a two-page document.

The style does not differ greatly from the UK but you will be expected to provide your date of birth, place of birth, nationality and marital status.

TOP TIP

If you're based in one country and your prospective employer is based in another country then you should endeavour to include international dialling codes with your phone and fax numbers.

PART 5

TAILORING YOUR CV

Whilst many people use a general CV designed to suit any position they are applying for, greater success can be achieved by tailoring your CV according to the needs of the specific role to which you are applying.

It is astonishing how many people use exactly the same CV for every single application they make.

It stands to reason that every job and every organisation is different, and every CV should therefore also be subtly different.

I could have discussed tailoring your CV with you earlier in this book, under the relevant chapters. However, I believe you will find it easier to create an initial 'master' CV, which you can then tweak and adapt as necessary rather than starting off by writing your CV with a specific vacancy in mind.

Some people will recommend that you should write your CV virtually from scratch for each and every application you make – but I think you'll agree that there are unfortunately not enough hours in the day!

Seeing the world from the recruiters' point of view

The recruiters' task is to identify the best matches between the vacancy and the candidates. They're not looking to find you the job that is best suited to you. They're looking to find a candidate that is best suited to their vacancy.

So you need to look at your CV from the recruiters' perspective. Instead of taking your skills and experience as the starting point, your starting point needs to be the requirements of the vacancy in question.

Too many people fall into the trap of focusing on themselves and not on the needs of their prospective employer. Recruiters are not interested in your life in and of itself! They are purely interested in whether or not there is a match between your background and the requirements of the role in question.

TOP TIP

If all your CVs are the same, then any statements you make are necessarily going to be generalised. What you actually need to do is carefully relate your skills and experience to those the recruiter is looking for.

You can even go beyond this and take a closer look at the organisation itself. What sort of organisation is it? What is its ethos? What sort of culture does it have? What type of people does it employ? Why do you want to work for this organisation in particular?

Is it really worth the effort?

Many people think this is all too much effort – or are scared that if they tailor their CV to a particular vacancy it might come across to the recruiter as if they've made too much effort to please.

As if it was possible to make too much effort!

On the contrary, surveys show that around a quarter of recruiters will in fact give preferential treatment to CVs that they feel have been tailored specifically to the vacancy in question. In a world where everyone is constantly bombarded with impersonal spam, the fact that you have taken the effort to tailor your application to better suit the vacancy in question will not go unrewarded.

For every advertised position there will be a considerable amount of competition. The employer could easily have over 100 applications to deal with. If you take a few minutes to tailor your CV (and cover letter) then the odds should increase very much in your favour.

A carefully targeted CV can easily mean the difference between success and failure.

Key words

If you have a job advert or description or person specification then an essential technique is to actually repeat back to them the 'key words' the recruiter has used. For example, let's say their advert states they are looking for:

> A creative and innovative individual able to manage their workload on their own initiative.

It would clearly be rather silly to repeat this verbatim straight back to them in your *Professional Profile*:

A creative and innovative individual, able to manage her workload on her own initiative.

That's not to say that a lot of people don't fall into this trap though!
You should instead aim to weave the key words into the overall flow of your CV. This is much more subtle – almost subliminal – but its effect should certainly not be underestimated.

EXAMPLE

A highly creative individual who excelled at university, gaining a 1st class BA (Hons) in Graphic Design. Most recently responsible for managing a heavy caseload on own initiative, liaising directly with clients to develop innovative solutions to their design needs.

By carefully mirroring the recruiter's own use of language you will definitely score points.

Which sections to tailor?

The *Professional Profile* and *Objective* sections are obviously ideal places to tailor your CV but you may still need to tweak other areas, such as the descriptions you have given in your *Career History*.

If you have included either a *Key Skills* and/or *Achievements* section then this might well benefit from some rewriting – or at least re-ordering – of the points you have raised.

In fact, these are not the only sections that might need tailoring; it all depends on the circumstances. If, for example, you are applying to work for a charity, even if it's not in a hands-on fundraising capacity, e.g. as an Administrative Assistant, then you might like to expand your *Interests and Activities* section so that it highlights some of your charitable interests.

Summary

> It is astonishing how many people use exactly the same CV for every single application they make.

> It stands to reason that every job and every organisation is different and every CV should therefore also be subtly different.

> You need to carefully relate your skills and experience to those the recruiter is looking for.

> Surveys show that around a quarter of recruiters will give preferential treatment to CVs that they feel have been tailored specifically to the vacancy in question.

> The best technique is to repeat back to the recruiter words that they have used in the job advert or description or person specification.

PART 6

DIGITAL CONSIDERATIONS

We live in an increasingly digital world and, as I mentioned earlier in this book, I readily expect you will possibly be making the majority of your applications by email (or fax) rather than by post.

Email and fax differ from good old-fashioned snail mail in a number of ways and I will be discussing these differences – and how to handle them – in this chapter.

I'd also like to discuss other ways in which technology might impact on your application, for example the rising use of scanning software.

And I'll conclude this chapter by discussing 'the future' – the future of CVs.

Faxing your application

Fax, is of course, less and less popular these days as a means of rapid document transmission. It has been totally overtaken by email. Nevertheless, some circumstances will still require an application to be submitted by fax and I am therefore occasionally asked how to deal with this.

One young lady recently asked me, 'Should I print the cover letter on the fax cover sheet or just do a normal letter and put a fax cover sheet on it?'

My recommendation would be to send the letter separately rather than including it on the fax cover sheet. Unlike an email, where the recipient has to open any attachments, the recipient of a fax hasn't got much choice but to see each and every page you are sending them. This gives you the opportunity to send a properly laid out and formatted letter rather than trying to scrunch your message up onto a fax cover sheet.

And what should you do if you don't get a reply? Should you follow up by sending yet another fax? Or is it better (assuming you have an address) to post your follow-up? This is another popular question.

My answer is that you would actually be much better off following up by telephone. You're not harassing the recruiter; you're simply politely enquiring to see if your fax has been safely received or not. Once you've got them on the phone they're much more likely to remember you when short-listing – and this is likely to work to your advantage. You stop being a random name and start becoming a real human being!

Emailing your application

Email is increasingly the preferred method of sending documents and it is perfectly possible that you will end up making the majority of your applications by email rather than by post.

You probably have a number of questions on your mind about emailing applications and I will try to answer all of these here.

Generally speaking, there's not too much difference between sending an application by post and sending an application by email:

> You still need to make an impact.

> You're still competing against countless others for the reader's attention.

> You still need to give them a compelling reason to read your CV (except that in this case they won't have it right there in front of them; they actually need to click to open it).

However, there are certain practicalities which you need to deal with:

Subject line: never leave it blank! It's extremely unprofessional to do so. But do keep it short and simple. You could specify the vacancy title and reference if applicable. If you're making a speculative application, on the other hand, then you might need to be a little more inventive and make a greater effort to catch the recipient's attention. Don't go over the top though; you certainly don't want to risk your email being labelled as spam and discarded.

Form of address: just because this is an email is no reason to start with 'Hi' or suchlike. Start your email just as you would start a proper, professional letter. This isn't an email to a pal; it's an important job application.

Content: whereas when faxing your CV and cover letter I would recommend sending the letter separately rather than including it on the fax cover sheet, I would definitely not recommend sending both your CV and cover letter as email attachments. The chances of either of them getting read will drop dramatically. I believe CVs should always be sent as attachments (because they normally look awful when copied and pasted into an email) but you should place the contents of your cover letter in the body of your email. (The exception to this is of course when a recruiter has specifically requested 'no attachments'.) By including any kind of attachment with your email you do run the risk of falling foul of spam filters. However, anti-spam software is becoming increasingly sophisticated and people are consequently becoming less paranoid about attachments they receive; not so long ago many companies had a policy of deleting all emails with attachments!

Signature: many people have an automated email 'signature' which goes out at the bottom of every email they send. Whatever yours says, remember that it will be seen by potential employers. You might decide a rewrite is in order!

Filenames: don't just call your CV 'CV'. Make sure it contains your name, e.g. 'Jane Bloggs – CV'. Organisations receive so many files simply called, 'CV'. It's easy for confusions to arise.

File format: Microsoft Word is the most universally accepted format for a document (apart from 'plain text' – which is really not very attractive). If you send your CV in a different format – PDF, Mac, etc. – then you're immediately reducing the chances of the recipient being able to access it (unless you work in a creative field, e.g. a graphic designer). Do you think the recipient will write politely back and ask for your CV in a different format? Or do you think it's more likely they will probably just delete your email?!

Cc and Bcc: in rare cases, where your application needs to be sent to more than one individual, then you might need to use the Cc function – and possibly even the Bcc function. However, it should go without saying that you shouldn't use these functions to spam multiple employers with exactly the same email. Each application you make should be tailored for the organisation to which you are sending it.

BLOOPER!

Be careful with your files and your filenames. I once received a file from a job applicant entitled, 'CV' which simply said:

what's at the bottom of my garden

Spider

Worm

Beetle

Bug

Needless to say, he didn't get the job.

Typefaces

We have already discussed typefaces, at the beginning of this book. However, I have some additional advice concerning CVs intended to be used primarily online.

First of all I need to define the difference between 'serif' and 'sans serif' typefaces.

A serif font has little flourishes or feet at the ends of some of the strokes that make up the letters and symbols within the typeface. And a sans serif font doesn't.

This is particularly noticeable on letters such as the capital 'W'. But really the easiest way to describe this is to show you:

This is a serif typeface. And this is a capital W. (Times New Roman)

This is a sans serif typeface. And this is a capital W. (Arial)

Can you see the difference?

Serif fonts are generally recommended for text which is physically printed and read on paper. They are considered to increase readability.

Sans serif fonts, on the other hand, are usually recommended for electronic use.

It can be a good idea to prepare two different versions of your CV – one using a serif font (e.g. Times New Roman) and the other using a sans serif font (e.g. Arial). You can then use one for applications you make by post or fax and the other for applications you make online or via email.

A recruiter receiving your CV by email may ultimately decide to print it but your first impression will normally be made 'on screen'.

CV databases and scanning software

Being bombarded with so many CVs, increasing numbers of organisations are turning to scanning and keyword-search software. This not only applies to CVs sent by email but also to CVs sent in as hard copies or faxed.

Scanning software has come along in leaps and bounds, and is now very adept at picking out CVs that best match the profile the user is targeting. If you have made an effort to write an outstanding CV from a human perspective, then it should also come across as an outstanding CV to scanning software. There is no point in creating a separate version specially adapted for scanning software. You have no idea whether or not the recipient will use scanning software so you have to cover every base in just one CV.

The advice I have already given you earlier in *The CV Book* as regards paper, fonts, etc. means that you will already have avoided most of the main traps you could have fallen into when it comes to scanning software. I also placed a lot of emphasis on the importance of your choice of words. However, I would reiterate that using appropriate keywords is of particular importance when it comes to 'impressing' scanning software. Part 5,

'Tailoring your CV', introduced you to the trick of weaving certain key words for the job advert into the text of your CV. The frequency with which such key words appear on a CV is a common short-listing criterion used by scanning software.

> **TOP TIP**
>
> ....
>
> You shouldn't get too obsessed with ways of ensuring your CV always come up tops on scanning software. As I say, if you create a powerful CV from the point of view of a human reader then it will more than likely be a powerful CV from the point of view of scanning software.

Security issues online

Whilst you should of course always be careful as to where you send such a personal document as your CV, special caution is advisable online.

It is all too easy for fraudsters to set up fake – yet thoroughly convincing – websites and invite people to submit their CVs for non-existent vacancies. Alternatively, they might claim to be new jobsites and suggest you upload your CV for their database.

I have already stated that highly personal details such as date of birth and marital status should never be included on CVs. Too few people realise the potential consequences if the personal information contained within their CV was to fall into the wrong hands.

I would also suggest you strongly consider removing the name of your current employer (if you are indeed currently in employment). You can replace it with a description such as 'small clothing retailer' or 'major High Street bank'.

Video CVs

There are those who think that written CVs are on their way out. Some claim that within the next decade the 'video cv' could become the standard. 'Will video kill the printed CV?', read one headline, suggesting that the advent of 'Web 2.0' and the 'YouTube Generation' means video CVs are very much the way forward.

Whilst research has shown that many employers react positively to the idea of a video CV, just as many see it as a gimmick. Not surprisingly, the sectors where video CVs are most popular are IT and sales/marketing – but even those employers who do react positively generally only see it as an additional tool to assist them in short-listing for interview. They still expect to see a proper, written CV.

Video CVs are very probably more than just a fad (their popularity has increased steadily over the past few years) but I certainly don't expect them to take the place of the traditional written CV any time soon.

Summary

> When sending an email, never leave your 'Subject' line blank. Specify the vacancy title and reference if applicable.

> Don't send both your CV and cover letter as email attachments. The contents of your cover letter should be placed in the body of your email.

> Don't just call the file for your CV 'CV'. Make sure it contains your name, e.g. 'Jane Bloggs – CV'. Organisations receive so many files simply called, 'CV'.

> If you have made an effort to write an outstanding CV from a human perspective then it should also come across as an outstanding CV to scanning software.

> For security reasons, highly personal details such as date of birth and marital status should never be included on CVs.

PART 7

A WORD ON ...

Chapter **16**

Cover letters

Cover letters are, according to a recent survey, seen by almost 50 per cent of recruiters as being equally as important as the CV itself, although most people spend the least amount of time on them.

So many people lose out on an interview not because of their CV but because of their cover letter. People are all too ready to blame their CV without giving a thought to their cover letter – yet it's frequently the cover letter that is to blame for the lack of success.

Never underestimate the importance of a cover letter

When someone has hundreds of CVs to plough through, the cover letter sets the tone of the application, and should inspire the reader to turn over enthusiastically and read the accompanying CV.

It is the ideal opportunity for you to succinctly summarise and re-emphasise the skills and experiences you have highlighted in your CV, while also giving you greater latitude to express your personality. It can help to focus attention on your strengths and distract attention away from any weaker points.

Get it wrong and you may find that the recruiter doesn't even bother to read your CV. Applications can be rejected solely on the basis of the cover letter.

Consequently, I would strongly recommend you take your time in preparing your cover letter – and maximise your chances of getting through to the interview stage.

The 15 most common cover letter mistakes – and how to avoid them!

The CV Centre has conducted a comprehensive analysis of over 1,000 cover letters to derive a 'Top 15' of the common mistakes people make.

1 Failing to write to the right person

The best person to whom to address your cover letter is clearly the person who is going to be making the decision as to whether or not to interview you. Too many letters are simply addressed to the 'HR Manager' and start, 'Dear Sir/Madam'. You want to try to get right through to the decision-maker. This is an elementary sales tactic but, unless you work within sales yourself, you're unlikely to be aware of how important it is to reach the person who actually has the power to make the decision you want them to make.

2 Not including your own full contact details

I would recommend that you start all your letters with a professional-looking letterhead. It is vital that the reader can spot, at a glance, not only your name but also precisely how to get in contact with you. Put your name at the very top, followed by your key contact details – address, phone number, email address, etc. Place your address on one line with your phone numbers on the next and finish with your email address. It's exactly the same as your CV.

3 Inappropriate email addresses

Whilst fun or jokey email addresses may be fine for corresponding with friends and family, employers will probably regard more 'serious' email addresses as simply more professional.

You might have taken time to put together a brilliant cover letter, but if your email address is mistressdominatrix@example.com then it may harm your chances!

4 Losing the reader's interest with your opening words

The primary goal of your opening paragraph is, of course, to explain to readers why it is that you are writing to them.

Yes, you're applying for a job – they'll figure that out pretty quickly. But why are you applying for this job? If you fail to start building your case immediately you risk losing readers' interest right from the very start.

5 Not saying what job you're looking for

At the beginning of your letter, you should always clearly state the position you are applying for along with any reference number(s) quoted in the job advert. It is very possible that recruiters will be simultaneously seeking candidates for various different positions, and it will make their life a lot easier if they can see clearly, at a glance, which vacancy it is that you are applying for.

6 Failing to make your case

Whilst it would definitely be a mistake to arrogantly oversell yourself, it is also a mistake to undersell yourself. Don't be afraid to blow your own trumpet and show a little self-confidence in what it is that you have to offer a prospective employer. It's a tight job market out there. You need to compete effectively if you're to stand any chance of achieving your career goals.

Make sure you give them compelling reasons to invite you for an interview.

7 Repeating what is written in your CV

Too many people fall into the trap of repeating too much of what their CV already says. This is not only likely to weaken the impact of the letter but may even put a recruiter off reading the CV.

A cover letter is an opportunity to draw the reader's attention to some of your key selling points – skills, experience, achievements – and to do so in a way which makes it clear how these will be of interest and potential benefit to the reader.

They've got a copy of your CV. Your cover letter should complement it – not repeat it. Your cover letter should introduce your CV – not replace it.

8 Lack of 'call to action'

The key to ending your letter is to make sure you do so in a positive, upbeat manner. You can't exactly demand a response from them – but you need to do everything in your power to encourage one.

This is where a little advertising device known as a 'call to action' comes in handy.

'Call to action' is a term used in advertising to describe a message to readers of an advert or other promotional material which is specifically designed to motivate them to take some specific action, perhaps pick up the phone and place an order, for example 'Call now while stocks last!'

You need to devise something similar to close your letter.

9 Talking about money before you've even got your foot in the door

You should certainly never voluntarily bring up the question of money in an initial cover letter. It can be a fatal mistake because it sends a clear message to the reader that you are more focused on your own needs than you are on theirs.

10 Giving the reader I-strain

The word 'I' is often over-used in cover letters. Unlike a CV, a cover letter should of course be written in the first person. However, if you start every sentence with 'I' then it can make for pretty tedious reading.

It might not be easy to cut down on your use of 'I' but you should definitely make an effort to do so. Look at each sentence which begins with 'I' and see if you can rephrase it so that it starts with a different word.

If you can turn around a sentence so that it starts, 'You' or 'Your' then this is ideal because it shows your focus is on the reader, not on yourself.

11 Lack of coherent structure

Like all the best stories, the best letters have a strong – and clearly defined – beginning, middle and end. It's important to make sure that your letter is structured in a logical fashion. Capture their attention, make an impact, maintain their interest and finish with a strong closing paragraph.

You've only got a certain amount of space – and a certain amount of words – to get your message across. If you don't structure your letter carefully then you'll end up rambling – and the impact of your letter will be severely diluted.

12 Length

As a general rule, most cover letters don't – and shouldn't – exceed one A4 page in length. Never lose sight of the fact that your cover letter is not intended to take the place of your CV; it's meant to act as an introduction.

Unless there are clear instructions to the contrary, you should aim to keep your letters short and sweet. A handful of paragraphs is normally more than sufficient to whet the recruiter's appetite and entice them to read your CV.

13 Spelling and grammatical errors

It might seem obvious. It might seem hard to believe that people actually do send out letters with errors in them. But, believe me, it happens all the time – and if you can make sure that your letters are totally error-free then you will immediately be at an advantage.

It is essential to check – and double check – that there aren't any spelling or grammatical errors, as this is most likely the recruiter's first impression of you. Make sure it's a positive one.

14 Spamming everyone with the same letter

In just the same way that your CV should ideally be tailored for each application, so should your cover letter. In fact, it is even more important to tailor your letter. A carefully targeted letter can easily mean the difference between success and failure.

It stands to reason that every job and every organisation is different, and every letter and every cover letter should therefore also be subtly different. If you send the same letter to everyone, changing only a few minor details such as name and address, then your chances of success will most definitely fall considerably.

15 Not signing the letter

Whilst you won't be able to physically sign a letter sent by email, you should always sign letters sent by post or by fax.

By taking the time to sign the letter before sending it, you're giving out one further signal to the reader that you have taken the time to write to them personally – and haven't just sent out the same letter to dozens of people.

My five top tips to make your cover letter stand out

Make an effort to accommodate these five points when writing your cover letter and you'll immediately be well above average.

1 Get through to the right person

The best person to whom to address your cover letter is the person who is going to be making the decision as to whether or not to interview you. Not only do letters addressed to a specific person achieve better results, but letters that actually reach the decision-maker have an even higher chance of making the grade.

2 Communicate clearly, concisely, engagingly and articulately

It is essential for your letter to be easy for the reader to scan quickly and effectively. Take your time to carefully phrase your thoughts; do not rush yourself. Make sure you get your message across.

3 Tell a good story

Like all the best stories, the best letters have a strong – and clearly defined – beginning, middle and end. It's important to make sure your letter is structured in a logical fashion. Capture the readers' attention, make an impact, maintain their interest and finish with a strong closing paragraph.

4 Target/tailor your letter

You should always tailor your letters according to the specific organisation to which you are applying. A carefully targeted letter can easily mean the difference between success and failure. Nobody likes being spammed.

5 Check your spelling and your grammar

Before sending off any letter, make sure you have read through it very carefully and that there are no spelling or grammatical errors. It's always a good idea to ask someone else to double-check for you.

Brilliant Cover Letters

If you would like to learn more about cover letters then please take a look at my comprehensive book on the subject, *Brilliant Cover Letters*. You can place your order for a copy via the following page on our website: **http://www.ineedacv.co.uk/brilliantcoverletters**

Chapter **17**

Application forms

It's a fact of life that not every employer will want a CV. Many larger organisations – particularly those in the public sector – will have standardised recruitment systems whereby candidates are required to complete an application form.

One of the main reasons for an employer to use application forms rather than accept CVs is that it is considered to be easier – and fairer – when comparing one candidate to another. It levels the playing field. CVs vary widely – from the brilliant right down to the outright absurd! However, by forcing every candidate to follow precisely the same format when presenting their details, the belief is that the quality of their CV is no longer a deciding factor in the recruitment process.

Another reason employers give is that, because it is time-consuming for a candidate to complete an application form, it reduces the number of applicants – in effect providing a form of pre-screening. The theory is that only those candidates who are really committed to the opportunity and who really think they have a chance will bother to take the time to apply.

Personally I am not a fan of application forms; I am not convinced by the arguments employers put forward for using them. I believe that requesting a CV with an accompanying cover letter is the best way to initially screen candidates for almost any role.

However, since you will no doubt come up against application forms during your job hunt, this chapter is here to help you tackle them as successfully as possible.

Guidance notes

Your most useful tools when completing an application form will normally have been provided by the employer themselves.

Application forms are normally accompanied by some form of guidance notes giving clear instructions as to what is expected from you. It is of the utmost importance that you follow any instructions to the letter.

Application packs will also commonly include a job description and/or person specification. These will give you a very clear picture of exactly what it is the employer is looking for – enabling you to complete the form accordingly. This will also give you the opportunity to weigh up whether it is really worth your while applying for the job. Do you really meet the criteria? There really is very little point spending precious time completing an application form for a job you don't stand a good chance of getting.

You should also take careful note of the submission deadline or closing date. If you can't get your completed form to the employer before this deadline then don't bother taking this application any further.

The application form

Most application forms follow the same basic pattern and largely follow the same format as a traditional CV:

> Personal Details
> Education and Qualifications (including Further Training)
> Career History
> Interests and Activities

In addition to these sections, most application forms have space for a 'personal statement' or ask a series of carefully designed 'competency questions' – and this is normally the greatest challenge the form presents.

It may also ask for details of referees as well as data required to ensure the equal opportunities policy is adhered to.

Below, we'll take a look at each of these sections, one by one.

Personal Details

This is normally very simple. Answer each question clearly and accurately – making sure you don't accidentally miss a question. Depending on how well (or badly) designed the form is, it can be surprisingly easy to overlook a question.

Education and Qualifications

Application forms normally require full details of all your qualifications including grades and, in the case of university degrees, often the specific modules you undertook.

If your application progresses then you might find the employer asks for copies of your certificates so it's obviously important to be as honest and accurate as possible when completing this section.

Whilst the format the employer has used may be geared towards UK qualifications, if your qualifications were gained abroad you should normally be able to make them fit. Many employers now use a qualification conversion table so, when assessing your application, they will be able to find the closest UK equivalents.

Career History

The level of detail required by the career history section varies widely from application form to application form.

Some forms will only request dates, job titles and organisation names. Others may want specific details of your duties, responsibilities and achievements – and maybe even your reasons for leaving.

If you're required to give a comprehensive description then do keep in mind the job description or person specification of the role for which you are applying. This is an important opportunity to demonstrate that you meet the criteria the employer has set out.

Interests and Activities

This should be very simple to complete and you can normally just copy details over from your CV. However, some forms might expect you to elaborate on your interests and activities more than you would normally do so when writing a CV.

Personal Statement

This is undoubtedly the most important part of an application form – and the only part that is likely to cause you any real difficulty.

The first step is to take a long, hard look at the job description and/or person specification. The onus is on you to demonstrate in your statement exactly how you meet the employer's criteria, so you need to make sure you understand very precisely what those criteria are.

It will help you to draw up a list of specific examples which you can use to illustrate the points you wish to make. Wherever possible you should try to integrate these real-world examples into your statement rather than just speaking hypothetically. Flagging up specific, relevant examples from your own experience is an ideal way of reinforcing your points in the reader's mind. You should be able to use your CV to help generate ideas.

When you come to putting pen to paper, you can either write using a paragraph structure as if you were writing a letter or you could try breaking up your statement using sub-headings. Unless you are given instructions to the contrary, the choice is yours. However, whichever approach you use

TOP TIP

Try to remember that the personal statement is not your enemy; it is your big opportunity to sell yourself and really make an impact. Use positive, engaging language and try to inject some life into what can otherwise be a rather dry block of prose. Approach your application form in an enthusiastic frame of mind and it is sure to reflect in your style of writing.

ensure that your statement progresses in a logical, methodical and ordered fashion, tackling each of the key issues one by one.

You will often be limited as to the number of words you are allowed to use – but by practising on a separate sheet (or word-processing document) first you can make sure you adhere to this requirement.

Competency questions

As an alternative to the personal statement (and sometimes in addition) application forms may contain a series of carefully worded questions designed to assess and analyse certain key competencies – and to ascertain precisely why you are applying for the role.

In many ways this is easier than completing a personal statement because the questions will steer you more precisely in the right direction. However, you should of course note that all applicants will have this same advantage.

In order to effectively handle such questions:

> Read through the question carefully to make sure you fully understand its meaning.

> Think about your answer in detail before you start trying to write it down.

> Ensure you cover all aspects of the question and don't miss anything.

> Endeavour to back-up your answers with appropriate examples from your own experience.

Referees

If an application form specifically asks for details of your referees then you will need to comply with this demand. Generally, you will be expected to provide details of at least two referees – usually one 'personal' and one 'professional'.

I would always recommend that you actually contact your potential referees before releasing their details. Not only do they need to be warned that they might be contacted but it's also polite to ask for their permission to release their details.

It may be quickest and easiest to just pick up the phone but in most cases a brief but courteous letter will be appreciated.

Miscellaneous formalities

Many employers now operate formal equal opportunities policies and, as part of this, you may be required to provide certain personal data regarding your ethnicity, etc. Make sure that you complete such details in full. Rest assured that it is illegal for an employer to use such data when making their selection.

You may also be required to consent to the use of your data in accordance with the Data Protection Act.

On paper or online?

Some employers will issue their application forms on paper others online – and some will give you the choice.

When completing an application form on paper:

> Practise first on a photocopy of the form, so as to ensure your answers fit the space available.

> Use a pen with black ink so that the employer can easily photocopy the form.

> Write as neatly as possible; it's vital that your writing be easy to read.

> Follow the instructions given; use block capitals where requested.

> Don't forget to sign and date the form if you're asked to do so.

> When you've finished, take a photocopy for use at interview.

When completing an application form online:

- If you're required to register first, keep a careful note of your log-in details.
- Type carefully – typing errors are not going to impress the reader.
- Make sure you adhere to any word count restrictions that might be imposed.
- Once you have completed the form, print a copy for your records if possible.
- Keep a careful note of any reference number you are given on submission of your form.

Check and double-check

In just the same way as you should always very thoroughly check any CVs or letters you send, you should also take time to read through your application forms. Any errors must be eliminated. A spelling or grammatical error in an application form could very possibly cost you the job – and all your efforts will have been wasted. If possible, ask a friend or family member to double-check for you.

Correcting errors is easy if you're completing your application form online. However, if you've made an error on your final copy of a paper-based form then you should correct it as neatly as possible, preferably using correction fluid.

My five top tips for application forms

Make an effort to take into account the following top tips when preparing your application form and you'll immediately be well above average.

1 Read, think and plan

Before you even consider putting pen to paper, make sure you have read carefully through any documents which accompany the application form – guidance notes, job description, person specification, etc. Ensure you also read right through the application form itself and that you fully understand all the questions.

2 Get yourself into the right frame of mind

Tedious it may be, but if you start writing your application form with a frown on your face then it's very likely to end up reflecting in your style of writing. Think positively, write positively and you stand a much better chance of making a positive impression on the reader. Sell yourself with enthusiasm.

3 Bring your application form to life with real-world examples

Wherever possible you should try to integrate real-world examples into your statement rather than just speaking hypothetically. Flagging up specific, relevant examples from your own experience is an ideal way of reinforcing your points in the reader's mind.

4 Check, double-check and check again

Before submitting your application form, make sure you have checked every last sentence and that there aren't any spelling or grammatical errors. Sometimes it's hard to see the wood from the trees and a fresh pair of eyes – a friend or family member – can spot errors you might have overlooked. You also want to be sure that you haven't missed a question.

5 Keep a copy for future reference

If you've got a paper-based application form, there's no excuse for not taking a photocopy once you've completed it. And even if you're completing the form online you should normally be able to print out what you've entered. If your application progresses to interview stage, then you will definitely find it very useful to be able to refer back to what you said originally.

Further application form resources

Please visit the following page on our website for further help with application forms: **http://www.ineedacv.co.uk/applicationforms**

Chapter **18**

Job hunting

If you can, cast your mind back to the dark days before the invention of the Internet ... Searching for a new job was definitely a lot more of an uphill struggle back then, involving hours and hours scanning the jobs pages, traipsing around recruitment agencies and posting countless CVs to countless employers.

With the creation of the Internet (and email), life has undoubtedly become a lot easier for a job hunter. However, while indeed very useful, the Internet is only one aspect of a balanced job hunt. In order to maximise your chances of success, you will also need to take into account all the more 'traditional' methods of finding a job.

In this chapter I will discuss the role the Internet should play in your job hunt and I will also cover the other main options at your disposal.

The Internet

There is little doubt that the Internet is now the single most important resource available to a job hunter. More and more employers are taking advantage of the Internet to satisfy their recruitment needs. It is therefore vital that you make the Internet one of your first ports of call.

There are thousands and thousands of job sites on the web, some very general, some specialising in particular lines of work, some specialising in recent graduates, some specialising in senior executives, etc., etc. (For links to specific resources please see 'Further reading and references'.) Both employers and recruitment agencies now make extensive use of such sites to advertise vacancies and to search for potential candidates.

Take the time to identify which job sites are most likely to be of use to you in your job hunt and then ensure you register with them and make the very most of what they have to offer. With so many sites out there, you could spend weeks going through them all, but I would recommend you be quite selective – there's probably only a dozen or so that really have the capacity to help you. However, it all depends on how much time you want to dedicate to this, because it's not going to cost you any more than your time – in almost all cases access is entirely free. It's the organisations advertising the vacancies and mining the database who provide the funding for these sites to operate.

The technology used by many sites is very sophisticated, enabling you to speedily locate vacancies which meet your specific requirements in terms of line of work, geographical area, salary range, etc. Other facilities include email alerts where, having fed your criteria into the system, you will be automatically notified by email of any new vacancies which might be of interest to you. But these are just a couple of features; on most sites there are usually many more. Job sites are constantly in severe competition with each other, and are always seeking to create and launch new facilities which will help their site users.

Whilst it definitely makes sense to concentrate on vacancies which have only recently been advertised (or for which the closing dates have not yet passed) it can be a surprisingly successful strategy to apply for older vacancies. There are many reasons why these vacancies might not yet have been filled – or might have been filled but the candidate didn't subsequently make it past their initial trial period.

As well as advertising vacancies on job sites, many employers will also have their own websites which can include details of vacancies they currently have on offer. Larger employers may even provide facilities for you to submit your application immediately online – either by completing a brief form and attaching your CV or by completing a full online application form.

Besides the above, all of the more 'traditional' methods of job hunting also now have an online element – and I will talk about each of these in turn.

Recruitment agencies

Recruitment agencies are, in my professional opinion, second only to the Internet in terms of their importance to you in your job hunt.

Most recruitment agencies also have a web presence, enabling you to quickly and efficiently locate agencies which might be appropriate for you. But I'd also recommend you have a quick look through your local *Yellow Pages* – that should give you a good overview of the agencies located more or less on your own doorstep.

A successful recruitment consultant will have an in-depth knowledge of the local job market and useful contacts with key local employers. Recruitment consultants have a vested financial interest in helping you to locate the job you want, so they are normally very committed to the task. Besides finding you a job they will also be very keen to help you to secure that job. They don't get paid unless you actually win the job! They will therefore be able to offer you a range of valuable advice, including helping you to negotiate your salary package.

You should aim to identify at least a handful of recruitment agencies which cater for candidates with backgrounds similar to your own – and then take the time to actually visit them in person. Like job sites, some recruitment agencies will specialise in particular sectors and others will be more general in their coverage; some will only handle permanent vacancies while others will also deal with temporary roles. Many recruitment agencies are small, local operations. However, there are a number of major national (and international) chains and, if these cover your line of work, then they should definitely be your primary target. They will typically have access to a much wider range of vacancies, not least because many employers will have an exclusive agreement with one agency – and only one.

Whilst there are undoubtedly many advantages of a face-to-face meeting with a real, live human being – and many recruitment agencies will insist on this – you should note that there are an increasing number of recruitment agencies which operate principally online, taking advantage of the Internet to broaden their market and reduce their High Street overhead. It would be a mistake to rule these out of your job search just because you're unable to meet with them in person.

Newspapers, magazines, journals, etc.

Even with the Internet at your fingertips, I'd strongly recommend you nevertheless take the time to trawl through newspapers (both local and national), magazines, trade journals, etc., which might contain job adverts of relevance to you.

Many jobseekers will be familiar with the process of flicking through the pages, circling possibilities and then short-listing vacancies for which they are actually going to apply. However, your life will be made easier by the fact that almost all publications now have websites with dedicated job sections. These will not only repeat most (if not all) of the adverts contained within the printed version of their publication, but they will often also carry additional adverts which only appear online.

The more prestigious publications are likely to have more advanced websites offering many of the same features as a major job site – sophisticated search facilities, email alerts, etc. It is, after all, in their interests for their advertisers to achieve a successful outcome – because it increases the chances of their paying for further advertising in the future.

Another facet of printed publications that is worth mentioning is that, apart from job adverts, they often contain a lot of useful background information on organisations. Even if an organisation isn't currently advertising a vacancy, you can make use of such information to submit a speculative application. Nothing ventured, nothing gained!

Speculative applications

As I say, nothing ventured, nothing gained. However, I believe speculative applications to be of much greater importance in a job hunt than most people give them credit for.

First of all, I'd like to clarify how I define a speculative application:

A speculative application is an application you make to prospective employers who have not openly stated that they have a specific vacancy they are keen to fill. You are simply contacting them to enquire whether or not they have opportunities for someone with your qualifications and experience.

It may sound a long shot – and I will admit that you probably will have a relatively low level of response – but if you have put together a strong CV and cover letter then you really are in with a chance. (In this particular case, the cover letter is especially important.)

Do you know how much an employer has to pay to advertise a vacancy in a national newspaper? And how much do you think a recruitment agency normally charges? Believe me, it's a lot of money! Any employer in their right mind will be keen to avoid such costs if it's practical to do so.

Even though they may not have any vacancies at the time of your initial application, they may well do so in the near future and, as long as your CV and cover letter make a powerful impression, you should hopefully be remembered when a suitable position does arise. You may still find yourself up against candidates supplied by a recruitment agency but the fact that you can essentially be recruited 'for free' may be a deciding factor, particularly for a small company.

Identifying suitable targets for speculative applications will require some research on your part but local (and national) newspapers, *Yellow Pages* and the Internet are generally the best places to start. Trade journals can also be very useful, not least because of the additional background information they can sometimes provide. However, having identified a target, it's not usually too difficult to dig up relevant information on the Internet – information you can use when crafting your cover letter.

Networking

Networking is – and always has been – a valuable job-hunting technique. I hired someone recently as a result of their applying through a mutual contact.

Networking takes many different forms and, for some people, it's almost an art form! It's also increasingly popular online with the advent of a wide range of social (and professional) networking sites.

Whatever means you use, if you are able to build up a network of contacts within your industry or sector, then the information they can provide could be very useful to your job hunt.

Networking can help you to identify vacancies before they're even advertised, as well as help you to identify possible targets for speculative applications.

Job fairs

Whilst attending job and career fairs can be time-consuming, it can also be extremely productive. In the space of a few hours you could have the opportunity to talk face-to-face with recruiters from dozens of different employers.

There's a whole multitude of different job fairs – some industry-specific, some targeting graduates, some only dealing with senior executives, etc. Use the Internet to identify those which might be appropriate for you. Your local Job Centre should also be able to provide you with such information.

When attending a job fair, make sure you dress as if you were attending an interview.

BLOOPER!

I have seen too many jobseekers walking around summer job fairs wearing T-shirt, shorts and flip-flops!

Most importantly, make sure you take a plentiful supply of CVs with you. Don't just take your CV on a memory stick and expect the recruiter to be able to download it – take actual printed copies.

Visit as many (appropriate) stands as possible and, politely but firmly, make contact with the individuals manning them. You're unlikely to be formally interviewed on the spot; this is all about making an initial approach and then, subsequently, building on that relationship. It's very much a form of networking. Collect business cards as if your life depended on it! Taking a large folder (or briefcase) with you is also advisable so as to help you physically cope with the quantity of corporate literature that will inevitably be thrust your way.

It's a numbers game

I'd like to conclude this chapter with an important tip.

If your CV is only being received by a handful of people per week, it could be that you're not getting your CV enough exposure for it to have an impact. As advertised positions often attract over 100 applications, on average one might conclude you need to make over 100 applications to secure the position you want.

That sounds a lot but, in reality, provided you have a strong CV and cover letter, the odds should increase very much in your favour. However, I won't hide the fact that finding the *right* job will most definitely require some work. But it will be worth it!

Further job-hunting resources

Please visit the following page on our website for further job-hunting resources. It contains a range of useful links to job sites and other online resources. I keep the list online because that way I can keep it bang up-to-date at all times: **http://www.ineedacv.co.uk/resources**

Keeping track of your job hunt

We've also put together a spreadsheet for you to help you keep track of the CVs you send out – who you've sent them to, what date, how you sent them (post/email/fax), etc.

Keeping track of your applications is important because following up can considerably increase the number of interviews to which you are invited.

This tracking tool will help you to know whether and when to follow up on an application and, quite simply, it will prevent you from becoming very confused! It's likely that you will need to send out dozens of CVs to secure the job you want and it's easy to get in a mess. Much better to keep yourself organised – and this Excel spreadsheet will enable you to do just that.

It's even got functionality to subsequently track your interviews.

To download your free copy, please visit the following link: **http://www.ineedacv.co.uk/tracker**

Chapter **19**

Interviews

Your application has been successful and you have been invited for interview; what next? People often think, well, I'll just turn up and be myself – which is fine, but it won't get you the job! You need to work hard to get yourself ready for an interview, as you are still up against many other applicants – and this is your key opportunity to make an impact.

Planning, preparation and organisation: a winning strategy

The best person for the job, in terms of the right skills, experience and achievements, doesn't always pass the interview. The best person for the job doesn't always get the job. Sometimes the most able candidates on paper can really shoot themselves in the foot when they actually get to the interview.

The interview is one of the most critical points in the job search process. Whilst you might look great on paper, you need to subsequently prove that in front of a hiring manager. Many other factors that are not related to the person's ability to do the job are going to be picked up in the interview.

You've got the skills; now you need to demonstrate clearly that you'll be a good fit with your future co-workers and employers – and it's so easy to sabotage this valuable opportunity if you're unprepared.

On average, there are likely to be at least five other candidates being interviewed for the same vacancy. So, everything else being equal, that gives you, at the most, a 20 per cent chance of getting the job. But there's so much you can do to improve your odds of success.

Pre-interview questionnaire

In order to help you plan and prepare for your interview I have developed the following brief questionnaire. It should help to get you thinking about all the most important issues you need to consider.

1 Regarding yourself and your interview history:
   (a) How many interviews have you attended within the past two years and how many of these have resulted in a job offer?
   (b) If any of your interviews failed to win you a job offer, why do you think that was?
   (c) What, if any, feedback have you received from an interviewer after an interview?

2 If you have won an interview for a specific role within a specific organisation:

(a) Have you applied for a position at this organisation before and/or what previous knowledge or experience of the organisation do you have?

(b) What is it about this particular position that appeals to you?

(c) If this position marks a change in career direction for you then why have you decided to make this change?

(d) What, if any, is your understanding/perception of the organisation's internal culture?

(e) What, if any, further information do you have with regard to the kind of skills and experience the organisation is looking for?

(f) Have you been asked to prepare a presentation and, if so, what instructions have you been given? e.g. content, time, visual aids to use, etc.

Interview scenarios: expect the unexpected

There are so many different kinds of interview. Here are some of the possible scenarios with which you might be faced:

> Classic one-on-one interviews

> Panel interviews

> Competency-based interviews

> Psychometric and aptitude tests

> Presentations

> Group interviews

> Assessment centres

> Telephone, video-conferencing and webcams.

Interview questions: and their answers!

While there are, of course, thousands of possible questions you could be asked, it's most important that you prepare thoroughly for following 'top ten'.

You should make sure you think very carefully through your answers to all these questions before getting anywhere near an interview room. Try to understand the meaning behind each question – what the interviewer's intentions are in asking you the question.

1 Tell me about your work experience – what did you do, what did you enjoy, what were you good at, why did you leave each job.

2 Why have you applied for this vacancy?

3 Why do you wish to leave your current position?

4 Why do you want to work for this organisation?

5 What are your strengths?

6 What are your weaknesses?

7 What has been your greatest achievement – in your personal life as well as in your career?

8 What can you, above all the other applicants, bring to this job?

9 Where do you see yourself in five years' time?

10 You've mentioned x under the *Interests and Activities* on your CV. Can you tell me a bit more about that?

You are absolutely certain to get asked at least some of these questions (or variations of them) if not the whole lot.

I could add an 11th question to the list: 'And do you have any questions for me/us?' There aren't many interviews that conclude without this question being asked – so you'll need to make sure you think of some good questions of your own to ask the interviewer.

My five top tips to interview success

Make an effort to accommodate the following and you'll immediately be well above average.

1 Be prepared

The key to preventing pre-interview jitters is preparation. If you are to be able to convince a recruiter that you are right for the role then you obviously first need to get it clear in your own mind why you are right for the role. As well as researching the job itself, you should also research the organisation.

2 Work through my pre-interview questionnaire

I would recommend you take the time to complete the questions above before any interview. It's only a short list of key questions but it should really help to get you thinking in the right direction.

3 Make sure you're there on time

Yes, it may seem so obvious, yet late arrival is consistently one of the very top reasons cited by recruiters for their rejecting candidates at interview stage. Don't be late. Better than that, aim to get there early so as to have time to relax and compose yourself.

4 Be confident and show your enthusiasm

Confident people inspire confidence in others – if you appear confident that you are able to do the job, the employer is likely to be more inclined to believe that you can – and showing a lack of enthusiasm is generally fatal to your chances of success. Be enthusiastic – and show it. Confidence and enthusiasm are traits that are guaranteed to impress an interviewer.

5 Don't recite your answers parrot-fashion

It's essential for you to think for yourself and to create your own answers to potential questions. Too many candidates make the mistake of sounding like they're reciting answers from an interview book. Even if you have prepared and memorised your own answers, you should be careful to make sure that your delivery is natural and doesn't come across as rehearsed.

The Interview Book

If you would like to learn more about interviews then please take a look at my comprehensive book on the subject, *The Interview Book*. You can place your order for a copy via the following page on our website: **http://www.ineedacv.co.uk/theinterviewbook**

PART 8

CV AND COVER LETTER EXAMPLES AND TEMPLATES

This chapter contains a selection of example CVs which should help to illustrate all the points made in this book – and which should also help you to generate lots of useful ideas for your own CV.

I start with the finished CV from our case study, Jane Bloggs, and then cover a variety of different professions, careers, sectors and circumstances.

Whilst these examples are based on real-life CVs which have helped my clients to win interviews, most of the fine details have been changed to preserve their anonymity and, in several cases, I have blended together several CVs so as to better demonstrate key principles. These CVs therefore don't represent real people and their real careers but they do represent the presentation, content, structure and style you should be aiming for when writing your own CV.

Free templates

These examples obviously include lots of formatting which it might be hard for you to copy from this book – or at the very least rather time-consuming to do so. I have therefore provided a special link for you to go online and download a full set of CV and cover letter templates. There's no charge for this. All readers of *The CV Book* are entitled to this entirely for free.

Simply visit the following page to quickly and easily download your free templates: **http://www.ineedacv.co.uk/freetemplates**

JANE BLOGGS

1 Any Road, Anytown AN1 1CV
Telephone: 01632 960 960 (Home); 07700 900 900 (Mobile)
Email: janebloggs@example.com

Professional Profile

A positive, proactive and results-driven Sales Manager with a proven track record of profitable business growth through the creation of successful sales and marketing strategies. Experienced in working with leading brands in the competitive food and drink sector, focusing on exceeding customer service expectations, ensuring optimum brand impact. Possesses excellent interpersonal, communication and negotiation skills and the ability to develop and maintain mutually beneficial relationships with key decision-makers.

Objective

Having successfully completed a BA (Hons) in Marketing and Advertising, now looking to return to the food and drink sector in a suitably challenging role. Keen to make best use of broad sales experience and strong theoretical knowledge of marketing and advertising.

Career Summary

2007–date   Sales Manager, ABC Stationery plc, London

- Playing a key role within a large stationery retailer, tasked with the redevelopment of the sales strategy across the UK market
- Planning and executing innovative campaigns, including direct mail and telesales
- Personally cold calling to bring on board high profile – and credit-worthy – new clients
- Liaising extensively with clients to agree product specifications, sale prices and lead times
- Building mutually beneficial relationships with suppliers, negotiating terms and discounts
- Interviewing, recruiting, training and mentoring new sales executives into the business
- Setting budgets and forecasting sales while maintaining full P&L accountability

Key Achievements

- Boosted regional sales levels by nearly 35% over a 2-year period with no additional marketing spend
- Organised a successful new product launch, gaining a substantial amount of local and national press coverage
- Featured in the programme, 'Business Lunch' on XYZ TV, providing invaluable exposure for the business

2001–2007   Sales Executive, XYZ Food plc, London

- Primarily tasked with account management, working closely with a small number of key clients
- Successfully pitching new products and lines, providing advice on effective visual merchandising
- Travelling extensively to meet with clients and help devise new strategies for boosting sales levels
- Actively responsible for financial issues such as credit control and resolution of bad debts

Key Achievements

- Led the introduction of a major culture change in customer service, improving customer satisfaction ratings from 6.2 out of 10 to 8.3 out of 10

Page 1 of 2

Career Summary cont.

1997–2001   **Marketing Assistant, MNO Drinks plc, London**

- Gaining valuable first experience of sales and marketing within a market-leading plc
- Assisting the Marketing Manager in the development of new campaigns and strategies
- Additionally liaising with external agencies and brand development consultants

Education and Qualifications

BA (Hons):   Marketing and Advertising, University of Sussex (2009)
3 A levels: English, English Literature and French (1997)
10 GCSEs: Including English and Mathematics (1995)

Further Skills

IT Skills: MS Office including PowerPoint & Access, QuarkXPress and PhotoShop
Languages: Fluent French; basic German

Further Training

- CLAIT Level 1: Including optional unit in Database Manipulation (2009)
- Commercial Awareness & Marketing Intelligence (2007)

Other Details

Driving Licence: Full/Clean
Health: Excellent; non-smoker

Interests and Activities

Currently include: Badminton, Squash and Pilates
                         Theatre (local 'amateur dramatics') and Cinema (especially classic films)

References are available on request

GRADUATE

Hannah Singh

1 Any Road, Anytown AN1 1CV
Telephone: 07700 900 389
Email: hannahsingh@example.com

Professional profile

A highly qualified MBA student with a unique combination of skills and capabilities acquired during studies and work experience. Able to demonstrate strong customer focus combined with a proven commitment to the achievement of targets and business objectives. Works effectively on own initiative with the organisation and time management required to complete assignments on time and to the required quality standard. Enjoys being part of a successful and productive team and thrives in highly pressurised and challenging working environments.

Objective

Currently looking to secure a marketing internship within a forward thinking organisation, one that will make best use of existing skills and experience while enabling further personal and professional development.

Education and qualifications

MBA:	Masters in Business Administration (Graduate October 2009) *MASTA London School of Business (accredited by University of Scotland)*
MSc:	Biotechnology (2007) *Paramedical College, Whalgar University, Calcutta, India*
BSc:	Biotechnology, Chemistry and Zoology (2005) *Kanpur University, Kanpur, India*
Intermediate:	Physics, Chemistry, Biology, English and Computer Science (2002)
High School:	Mathematics, Science, Social Science, English and Hindi (2000)

Further skills

I.T. Proficiency:	Word, Excel, C++, Internet and Email
Languages:	Fluent English and Hindi; currently learning French

Work experience

2007–2009　　　　**Customer Care Officer, Pensions R Us Ltd**

- Providing information and advice to employees of several major US hotel chains regarding their pensions plans
- Advising on the availability of suitable pension plans and assisting with the transfer of plans from one fund to another

Interests and activities

Currently include:	Photography, Drawing, Reading (autobiographies and science journals), Swimming, Football and Badminton

References are available on request

Hannah Florence

1 Any Road, Anytown AN1 1CV
Telephone: 01632 960 227 (Home); 07700 900 956 (Mobile)
Email: hannahflorence@example.com

PROFESSIONAL PROFILE

An enthusiastic and versatile professional, with strong practical experience in nursing practice within a multi-disciplinary environment and an acute surgical setting, specialising in emergency, elective bowel surgery and vascular surgery. A focused and proactive person adopting a motivated and positive approach to all tasks, with a commitment to deliver the highest standards of patient care at all times. Possesses excellent interpersonal and communication skills with the ability to adapt to any situation and prioritise tasks. Key assets are strong attention to detail, the ability to communicate with patients, families and staff at all levels and a natural facility to work under pressure.

EDUCATION AND QUALIFICATIONS

2009:	Vac-KCI Wound Management
	ALERT
	Immediate Life Support
2008:	Diploma in Adult Nursing
	Adult Protection
2003:	8 GCSEs (including English and Mathematics)

PROFESSIONAL TRAINING

- Intravenous Administration
- Fresenius Volumetric and Syringe Pumps
- Setting up PCAs
- PICC and Central Venous Catheter Use

CAREER SUMMARY

2008–date *Staff Nurse, Curie Ward – Royal Hampshire Hospital*

- Assessing patient care needs and the development, implementation and evaluation of care programmes
- Assisting in the systematic monitoring and evaluation of nursing practice and implementing standards of patient care supported by solid evidence-based results
- Ensuring all nursing practices comply with the Trust's Nursing policies and procedures including the NMC Code of Conduct, maintaining the highest possible standards
- Developing and maintaining strong working relationships with health care staff, medical staff and other members of the primary care and social services teams in order to deliver outstanding patient care
- Managing a small case-load of patients and coordinating and monitoring individual patients progress along their critical trail
- Actively supporting the implementation and maintenance of Team Nursing within the clinical area and organising patient discharges
- Ensuring all matters regarding the implementation of clinical governance are addressed on the unit including the regular maintenance and evaluation of care standards
- Providing a prompt and appropriate response to complex enquiries and complaints from staff, patients and members of the public in order to prevent any formal complaints
- Responsible for intermittently acting as the 'nurse in charge' under the direct supervision of a senior staff member and coordinating shifts and appropriately deploying staff in line with Trust Guidelines
- Conducting regular ward audits and maintaining an adequate supply of all required equipment and linen in the absence of the Ward Manager

INTERESTS AND ACTIVITIES

Currently include: Reading, Swimming and Dog Walking & Training

REFERENCES ARE AVAILABLE ON REQUEST

Richard Vermont

1 Any Road, Anytown AN1 1CV
Telephone: 07700 900 629
Email: richardvermont@example.com

PROFESSIONAL PROFILE

A dedicated and compassionate medical professional who specialises in the field of spinal neurosurgery. Able to demonstrate strong clinical expertise with the proven ability to assess and investigate patient symptoms and make appropriate decisions on the most appropriate treatment accordingly. Committed to the field of research and development with the aim of improving standards of medical practice through the use of technological advances. A valuable member, and leader, of a successful multi-disciplinary team who thrives in highly pressurised and challenging working environments.

EDUCATION AND QUALIFICATIONS

2006:	Doctorate of Medicine in Neurosurgery, University of Jamaica
	European Final Board Examination in Neurosurgery – Jordan Diploma & Prize
2005:	European Primary Board Examination in Neurosurgery
2004:	Final Intercollegiate Fellowship in Neurosurgery
	Fellow of the Royal College of Surgeons of England
2000:	Doctor of Medicine Part I, University of Jamaica
1996:	MBBS with Honours, University of Jamaica

AFFILIATIONS

- General Medical Council UK (9727294)
- Medical Council of Jamaica (9264)
- Educational Commission for Foreign Medical Graduates, USA (1-934-423-2)
- Member of the Society of British Neurological Surgeons
- Member of the European Association of Neurosurgical Societies
- Fellow of the Royal College of Surgeons of England
- Fellow of the Caribbean College of Surgeons
- Member of the British Medical Association
- Member of the Jamaica Medical Doctors Association
- Member of the Medical Association of Jamaica

PROFESSIONAL DEVELOPMENT

- IELTS
- Communication Skills Course
- OSCE Examiner Workshop
- Epidemiology Workshop
- Advanced Trauma Life Support Certification
- Advanced Cardiac Life Support Certification
- Ultrasonic Aspirator
- Tissue Vaporizer
- Basic Life Support Certification
- Advanced International Microsurgical Anatomy Course
- Advanced Pneumatic Instrumentation Medtronic Midas Rex
- Leeds Spine Study Day

ACHIEVEMENTS

- VIP Pelican, University of Jamaica – Alumni Magazine (2008)
- Jordan Prize for Best Performance in Final European Board Examination in Neurosurgery, Luxembourg (2007)
- Second Place in the European Primary Board Examination in Neurosurgery, Finland (2006)
- Best Performance in the Doctor of Medicine in Surgery Part 1 Examination (2000)
- Jolbury Prize in Medicine for Best Performance in Medicine and Therapeutics in the final MBBS Exam (1996)
- Pfizer Clinical Medicine Award for Best Performance in the Clinical Station in Medicine (1996)
- David Bleak Prize in Anatomy, First Stage MBBS Exam (1993)

CONSULTANT APPOINTMENTS

- The Einstein Memorial Hospital (2006)
- The Lisa Institute of Medical Sciences (2006)
- The University Hospital of Jamaica – Honorary (2006)

Page 1 of 4

CAREER SUMMARY

Current   **THE ESSEX NEUROLOGICAL CENTRE, EXETER GENERAL HOSPITAL**
Locum Consultant Spinal Surgeon – Department of Neurosciences

- Playing a pivotal role in the development of the spinal service at the Exeter General Hospital while setting up research and audits relevant to the specific area of practice
- Participating in the on-call emergency rotas for both neurosurgical and spinal as well as conducting routine outpatient clinics, special A&E clinics for semi-urgent referrals and outreach clinics to local district general hospitals
- Managing a full day operating list while also attending weekly spinal MTD meetings and departmental governance meetings
- Providing advice and specialist services to local GPs and other medical professionals as well as supervising neurosurgical trainees

2008   **THE SIMPSON CENTRE FOR NEUROLOGY & NEUROSURGERY**
Senior Spinal Fellow

- Conducting pre-operative and post-operative assessment of in-patients and out-patients before assisting with operations both independently and under supervision of the Consultant
- Building rapport with adult and paediatric patients and their relatives and ensuring their full understanding of the neurosurgical conditions
- Playing a key role as second-in-line within a multi-disciplinary team with responsibility for the supervision of junior staff, registrars and ST trainees
- Adopting a collaborative approach to patient care by working in close conjunction with nursing, physiotherapy and occupational therapy staff
- Additionally liaising with neuroanaesthetic, neuroradiology, neurology and neuropathology colleagues regarding the conditions affecting patients
- Participating in a 1:13 on-call service covering adult patients at the Simpson Centre and paediatric emergencies at the Royal Manchester Children's Hospital
- Handling on-call referrals from Doctors in district hospitals and GPs, assessing the clinical details and radiological imaging and discussing the patient with the Consultant before making a decision on the next course of action
- Admitting patients when required and informing Bed Managers of the level of priority for each particular patient
- Playing a key role as Spinal Fellow at the Royal Leeds University Hospital with full involvement in adult operations
- Responsible for teaching junior neurosurgical trainees and medical students to facilitate their professional development
- Attending weekly MDT meetings for spinal surgery, radiology and oncology and participating in clinical audits and research

05/2005–06/2006   **UNIVERSITY HOSPITAL OF JAMAICA**
Senior Registrar – Neurosurgery

03/2003–04/2005   **SLOUGH GENERAL INFIRMARY**
Senior Registrar / Registrar – Neurosurgery

01/2003–02/2003   **UNIVERSITY HOSPITAL OF JAMAICA**
Registrar – Neurosurgery

TEACHING EXPERIENCE

Teaching
- Lecturer, Leeds University (Pending Appointment)
- Lecturer, Faculty of Medical Sciences, University of Jamaica (2006–2008)
- Teaching neuroscience, neuroanatomy, neurology, neurosurgery to medical students, surgical trainees, junior residents, SHOs, postgraduate residents and nursing staff
- Personally requested by the Dean of the Faculty of Medical Sciences to teach neuroanatomy to second year medical students in the Department of Basic Medical Sciences, University of Jamaica

Examining
- Examiner for the Accident & Emergency Nurses Training Programme, University Hospital of Jamaica (2006)
- Examiner for Second Year Physiotherapy Students, University Hospital of Jamaica
- Examiner for Second and Third Year Medical Students in Anatomy, University Hospital of Jamaica
- OSCE Examiner for the University of Manchester Medical Students

RESEARCH AND PROJECTS

Fields of Research
- Neuromicrosurgical Anatomy; Microsurgical Anatomy Lab; Hydrocephalus; Surgical Oncology

Externally Funded Projects
- Acquisition of a New Midas Rex Drill from Medtronic, valued at $30,000 (2001)
- $3,000 grant from Codman, Johnson & Johnson towards the development of the surgical residents group
- Medtronic and Carl Zeiss sponsorship ($15,000) of an International Microsurgical Anatomy course conducted by Professor Jane Sampson (2004)

Publications
- *The Management of Spinal Dural Arterio-Venous Fistulas at The Simpson Centre 2000–2007* (Pending)
- Management of malignant metastatic spinal cord compression – *British Journal of Neurosurgery* (2009)
- Pure subdural haemorrhage from a ruptured Pcom Aneurysm – commentary *WIMJ* (2004)

Presentations
- *Endoscopic Third Ventriculostomy* – Caribbean Neuroscience Symposium, Lisa (2004)
- *Approaches to the Anterior Cervical Spine* – Caribbean Neuroscience Symposium, Lisa (2003)
- *C-Section at the University Hospital of Jamaica – Too Few or Too Many?* – Second Medical Faculty Research Day Conference (1994)

Operative Videos Recorded, Edited and Produced
- Craniotomy and clipping of Left Middle cerebral artery aneurysm
- Clipping of a giant basilar superior cerebellar artery aneurysm via a half and half approach
- Craniotomy and clipping of a PCOM aneurysm
- Craniotomy and clipping of a Rt MCA aneurysm
- Endoscopic third ventriculostomy
- Endoscopic third ventriculostomy
- Bifrontal craniotomy and resection of craniopharyngioma
- RT Fronto-temporor-orbital craniotomy and resection of craniopharyngioma
- Transphenoidal resection of pituitary adenoma
- Endoscopically assisted resection of pituitary adenoma
- Lumbar microdiscectomy L4/5
- Frontal craniotomy and transcortical resection of a SEGA tumour
- Endocscopic third ventriculostomy for posterior fossa tumour
- Endoscopic third ventriculostomy for suprasellar cyst
- Endoscopic third ventriculostomy for post fossa tumour
- Endoscopic third ventriculostomy for post fossa colonic metastasis
- Post fossa craniotomy and resection of medulloblastoma
- Post fossa craniotomy and resection of astrocytoma
- Insertion of syringo-peritoneal shunt for trauma associated syrinx
- Insertion of syringo-peritoneal shunt for tumour associated syrinx
- Craniocervical decompression for chiari 1 malformation without syrinx
- Craniocervical decompression for chiari 1 malformation with syrinx
- Anterior cervical decompression for cervical spondylitic myelopathy
- Orbito-zygomatic craniotomy, pit adenoma and frontal astrocytoma – composite video of image guided surgery at the UHWI
- Clipping of PCOM aneurysm
- Craniotomy & resection of temporal AVM
- Craniotomy & clipping of MCA and ACOM aneurysm
- Craniotomy and clipping of PICA aneurysm
- Craniotomy and resection of Colloid cyst
- Occipital–transtentorial resection of a pineal region astrocytoma
- Endoscopic third ventriculostomy for post fossa ependymoma
- Endoscopic third ventriculostomy for pineal region metastasis
- Anterior cervical microdiscectomy and plating

Development Projects
- Participating in the development of a surgical laboratory at the University Hospital of Jamaica
- Developing a website for the surgical residents groups at the University Hospital of Jamaica

CONFERENCES AND TRAINING

- SBNS Meeting
- European Association of Neurosurgical Societies
- Specialist Fellowship Exam Course
- OSCE Workshop
- Second Caribbean Neuroscience Conference
- First Leeds Aneurysm Surgery Course
- Minimally Invasive Courses
- Inaugural Caribbean Neuroscience Symposium
- Biostatics Workshop
- Ena Thomas Symposium
- Medical Association of Jamaica Conferences
- Biostatistics Seminar
- Temporal Bone Dissection Course

- Microsurgical Anatomy
- Peripheral Nerve Course
- Brain Mapping Course
- Skull Base Approaches
- Endoscopic Pituitary Course
- Microsurgical Anatomy
- Traatek Instrument Training
- Dr Ruth's Microsurgical Anatomy Course
- Minimal Approaches to the Lumbar Spine
- Midas Rex Course
- Society of British Neurosurgical Surgeons
- American Association of Neurological Surgeons
- Congress of Neurological Surgeons USA

FURTHER SKILLS

I.T. Proficiency: Word, Excel, PhotoStudio, Movie Maker, MGI Video Wave Movie Maker and I-photo
Languages: Basic French and Spanish

PERSONAL DETAILS

Driving Licence: Full/Clean
Interests include: Football, Cricket, Athletics, Theatre, Photography, Video Editing and Production

REFERENCES

Mr Paul van Hille

Consultant Neurosurgeon

The Walford Centre
Manchester
UK

Mr Philip von Halle

Consultant Neurosurgeon

Bradford General Infirmary
Bradford
UK

Mr James Holness

Consultant Neurosurgeon

Bradford General Infirmary
Bradford
UK

Mr Albert Infield

Consultant Neurosurgeon

Bradford General Infirmary
Bradford
UK

Professor Albert Johnson

Neurosurgeon

Haptassie University
Canada

Professor Derek Billmore

Neurosurgeon

University of Miami
Miami, Florida
USA

ESTA MORRIS
1 Any Road, Anytown AN1 1CV
Telephone: 07700 900 362
Email: estamorris@example.com

PROFESSIONAL PROFILE

A resourceful, hard-working and dedicated Electronics Engineer and Physical Scientist with an outstanding academic background, a good publication record and significant experience in the design and development of digital and analogue circuits, PLC circuit programming, UHF and HF radars and optical imaging equipment. Possesses excellent presentation skills and can prepare comprehensive documentation and reports as required. Experienced in data processing, is quick to grasp new ideas, technologies and concepts, and is skilled in a range of industry-standard software packages. Works well both independently and as part of a team, demonstrating the motivation and organisation required to meet demanding targets. Combines an analytical and professional approach with excellent interpersonal skills and can communicate concisely at all levels.

OBJECTIVE

Now looking for a new and challenging position, one that will make best use of existing skills and experience and provide opportunity for further responsibility and professional development.

CAREER SUMMARY

2007–date   ***Postdoctoral Research Assistant, University of Reading***

- Undertaking enzyme engineering, including cloning, mutagenesis, fermentation, expression, purification and characterisation
- Developing a novel expression system to increase the productivity of Putidaredoxin Reductase ten-fold and transferring the entire production procedure to a commercial basis
- Synthesising fine chemicals by biotransformation using recombinant cells with cytochrome P450 enzymes
- Producing a dehydrogenase end-point reaction platform for further development into a biochemical analysis kit
- Development of electrochemical biosensors for total cholesterol, HDL and total triglycerides, including optimisation of HDL chemistry and development of an immuno-sensor combined with EMIT, writing assay protocols and carrying out protein modification, lyophilisation, immunoassay and ELISA

2002–2005   ***Research Assistant, Department of Communications Systems, Basingstoke University***

- Undertaking programming and ensuring the effective operation of UHF radars and HF transmitters in remote sensing research
- Carrying out detailed and cutting-edge signal and image processing activities in order to investigate HF-induced artificial auroras

- Supervising and providing guidance on a number of MSc projects covering RF circuit design, digital signal processing and satellite systems

EDUCATION AND QUALIFICATIONS

2002–2006: PhD, Space Plasma Environment and Radio Science
Thesis 'Radio and Optical Observations of Natural and Artificially Stimulated Geo-space Plasmas'

1996–2001: BSc Electronics/Communications Engineering
Modules include Electrical Circuits, Electronics, Logic Circuits, Control Systems and Automation, Telecommunication Theory and Circuits, Electromagnetism, Antennas, Microwave Circuits
Final Year Project 'Design and construction of wireless multi-channel handsets for voice and data communication'

AWARDS

Royal Astronomical Society prize for best presentation in National Astronomy Meeting (2009)

TECHNICAL SKILLS

- *Fermentation engineering*
- *Bioanalysis development*
- *Biosensor Development*
- *PCR, UV/VIS, SDS-PAGE*
- *AUTOLAB*
- *Enzyme engineering*
- *Biosynthesis development*
- *HPLC, FPLC, GC, MS*
- *EMIT, ELISA*
- *Lyophilisation*

PUBLICATIONS

E.A. Bentley, Y. Astier, E. Morris, S.G. Bell, L.L. Wong, H.A.O. Hill. *Inorgania Chimica Acta.* 2005; 356 (347–348)

E. Morris, C. Yili, and W. Wu. Properties of Cholesterol Oxidase from Brevibacterium. The 4th International Conference of Food Science and Technology, Wuxi, China. 2004; 10 (79–80)

E. Morris, C. Yili, Z. Hechun and W. Wu. Purification and Properties of Cholesterol Oxidase from Brevibacterium. 3rd Symposium for National Young Microbiologist. Wuxi, China. May 29, 2004

E. Morris, C. Yili, Z. Hechun and W. Wu. Colorimetric Determination of the Activity of Cholesterol Oxidase. University of Light Industry. 2003

PERSONAL DETAILS

Driving Licence: Full/Clean
Health: Excellent; non-smoker
Work Permit: Full UK work permit

Amanda Whittle

1 Any Road, Anytown AN1 1CV
Telephone: 01632 960 828 (Home); 07700 900 219 (Mobile)
Email: amandawhittle@example.com

PROFESSIONAL PROFILE

An enthusiastic and dedicated legal graduate who enjoys being part of a successful and productive team. A confident and articulate communicator with a professional manner and the ability to conduct impressive and persuasive presentations and work of the highest quality. Extremely organised and highly self-motivated, with a proven background in achieving targets and meeting tight deadlines, performing well in a highly pressurised working environment. Possessing excellent interpersonal and liaison skills with the ability to communicate professionally with customers and encourage colleagues, building and maintaining productive working relationships.

OBJECTIVE

Now looking for a new and challenging position in legal profession that will make best use of existing skills and academic achievements enabling further personal and professional development.

EDUCATION AND QUALIFICATIONS

LLM: **Business and Commercial Law** – *Result Pending*
    2008–2009
        Julius Jenkins University, Manchester
        Modules:

- ➢ Business and Social Organisations
- ➢ Employment Law
- ➢ Commercial Leases
- ➢ Corporate Governance
- ➢ ADR
- ➢ Commercial Contracting

LLB (Hons.):   **Law** – *2:1*
    2005–2008
        Julius Jenkins University, Manchester
        Modules:

- ➢ Public International Law
- ➢ Succession Law
- ➢ United Nations International Security Law
- ➢ Land Law
- ➢ Obligations B (Contract and Tort)
- ➢ Introduction to Business Organisations
- ➢ Introduction to Employment Law
- ➢ Obligations A (Contract and Tort)
- ➢ Foundations
- ➢ Family Law
- ➢ Employment Law
- ➢ Financial Crime
- ➢ Equity & Trusts
- ➢ EU Procedural Law
- ➢ Property Offences
- ➢ Criminal Law
- ➢ Public Law
- ➢ Legal Research

Diploma: **Law** – *2:1*
    2003–2005
        Intercollege, Nicosia-Cyprus
        Modules:

- ➢ Professional English of Law
- ➢ English Composition
- ➢ Criminal Law I-II
- ➢ English Legal System I-II
- ➢ Basic Writing
- ➢ Microcomputer Applications
- ➢ Contract Law I-II

EDUCATION AND QUALIFICATIONS cont.

High School: **Prianpancy Lyceum Larnaca (Cyprus)**
2000–2003

Modules:
- Classical Greek
- Latin
- Philosophy
- French
- Modern Greek
- History
- English

FURTHER SKILLS

IT Proficiency: Working knowledge of Windows 98/2000/XP/Vista
Expert knowledge of MS Office 98/200/XP/2003/2007

Languages: Greek (native) and English (fluent)

WORK EXPERIENCE

2007–2009 Part-time Teacher – *Manchester's Greek School*
- Financially supported studies offering comprehensive teaching service to students of Liverpool's Greek School including devising innovative lesson plans and teaching strategies
- Gaining experience of effective time and manpower management, addressing queries and issues raised by parents and students and liaising with fellow staff members

2004–2005 Bar Staff – *Grand National, Aintree Racecourse*
- Dynamic and multifaceted role providing professional customer services in sale of food and beverages to patrons
- Developed excellent interpersonal and communication skills interacting with staff and customers remaining affable and focused at all times
- Worked as part of a team to coordinate bar duties in prompt, effective manner

2003–2006 Assistant – *Marathon Tours, Larnaca, Cyprus*
- Offered assistance and gained experience within tourism industry dealing with general enquiries and general administration including ticketing and invoicing

PERSONAL DETAILS

Driving Licence: Full/clean
Health: Excellent; non-smoker
Sports Interests: Prior member of High School Basketball Team, three times Cyprus Champions; Represented Cyprus in World Championship in Turkey and Hellenic Championship
General Interests: Fashion, Cooking and Dance
Specialised Interests: Vice-Chairperson for two years and then Chairperson of the Greek–Cypriot Society between 2005–2009
Participation in Youth Exchange Seminar for European Union in Italy, Portugal, Poland, Greece, Hungary and Cyprus

REFERENCES ARE AVAILABLE ON REQUEST

Robert Ward

1 Any Road, Anytown AN1 1CV
Telephone: 01632 960 238
Email: robertward@example.com

PROFESSIONAL PROFILE

A versatile and dynamic professional with a successful background delivering substantial improvements in standards of teaching and learning. A competent strategist with the proven ability to influence policy and developments to enable a direct impact on children's education. Possesses excellent interpersonal, communication and negotiation skills and the ability to develop mutually beneficial partnerships both internally and externally. A motivational and inspirational leader capable of coaching and empowering teaching staff to enable them to fulfil their potential whilst ensuring that they make a positive contribution to the achievement of objectives.

CAREER SUMMARY

2006-date　　　　**SPECIALIST SCHOOLING TRUST, LONDON**
　　　　　　　　　　Designation Management Coordinator

- Managing the dedicated team of 11 staff responsible for advising schools on designation and re-designation as specialist schools with a budget of £3.5 million
- Establishing and maintaining mutually beneficial relationships with DCSF, TDA and YST including working with DCSF regarding policy decisions for specialist schools
- Playing a pivotal role in the formulation of new policies, the preparation of bids and the management of £400K of commercial activities
- Producing comprehensive on-line guidance documents for schools as well as creating professional development courses and delivering the same to middle leaders
- Preparing and delivering highly effective presentations to senior staff in schools across the country whilst also presenting seminars to school governors

Key Achievements
- Actively involved in a major change initiative to the re-designation process involving informing schools, training staff and providing feedback to DCSF

1996-2006　　　　**ORANGEMORE COLLEGE, PORTSMOUTH**

2000-2006　　　　**Assistant Principal / Vice Principal**
- Fully accountable for Curriculum Development within the school and for driving improvements in teaching and learning whilst controlling the annual budget of £400K
- Playing a lead role in encouraging the strategic utilisation of ICT within all areas of the curriculum
- Providing management and support to Assistant Principals and Advanced Skills Teachers and contributing to their professional development

Key Achievements
- Personally responsible for the management of three successful re-designation bids for specialist status whilst also successfully achieving Training School status
- Winning numerous grant awards and sponsorships as a direct result of managing negotiation processes with local companies
- Contributing directly to the school moving from 35% 5 A*-Cs to 50% whilst in charge of teaching and learning
- Winning the Granada Award for Schools Work in the Community in recognition for community work undertaken at the College

1996-2000　　　　**Head of Humanities & ICT Coordinator**
- Responsible for the management of the humanities faculty whilst coordinating the delivery of ICT across the curriculum

Key Achievements
- Leading the strategic development of ICT and overseeing major developments and purchases
- Managing the introduction of one of the first school remote access facilities in the country as well as coordinating DCSF funded video conferencing projects
- Developing new courses within Humanities with considerable success enjoyed in examination results

Page 1 of 2

CAREER SUMMARY cont.

1989-1996   **WATERGATE COMMUNITY COLLEGE, WATERGATE**
Head of Humanities & Professional Mentor

- Managing the Initial Teacher Training & Professional Development and initiating the mentoring programme for trainee teachers

Key Achievements
- Writing and implementing a new appraisal policy to facilitate substantial improvements in performance management
- Making a significant personal contribution to curriculum development using cross-curricular themes
- Leading the College's environmental work resulting in it winning the Radio Solent's Environmental Challenge in 1996

1980-1989   **THE QUEEN'S SCHOOL, NEWTOWN**
i/c Lower School Humanities

- Successfully coordinating disparate members of staff from different departments to deliver an integrated humanities course covering history, geography and RE

Key Achievements
- Spearheading the development of resources including the use of visual-audio and information technology

EDUCATION AND QUALIFICATIONS

NPQH: National Professional Qualification for Headship
PGCE: Geography
BA (Hons):   Geography – 2:1
3 A Levels: English, French and Geography
8 O Levels: Including English and Mathematics

PROFESSIONAL DEVELOPMENT

- Ofsted and Inspection Framework (Key Note Speaker)
- Raise Online
- SSAT's Data Enabler Toolkit
- Certificate in Further Professional Studies

PUBLICATIONS

- Globalising the Curriculum (published in Teaching History, AG Publications, September 2008)

FURTHER SKILLS

I.T. Proficiency: Word, Excel, Access, Fireworks, Publisher, Photoshop, Internet and Email
Languages: Intermediate French

INTERESTS AND ACTIVITIES

Currently include: Hill Walking, Football, Cricket, Rugby Union and Reading (Classics & History)

REFERENCES ARE AVAILABLE ON REQUEST

Gareth Hobson

1 Any Road, Anytown AN1 1CV
Telephone: 07700 900 235
Email: garethhobson@example.com

PROFESSIONAL PROFILE

A dedicated and dynamic professional combining strong business acumen with extensive experience in managing internal and external audit processes. Attentive to detail with a logical and analytical approach to solving complex problems and issues. Able to demonstrate an excellent knowledge of Sarbanes Oxley, UK and US GAAP regulations with the proven ability to ensure full compliance therewith while also being proficient in internal audit and business processes. Possesses excellent interpersonal, communication and negotiation skills, the ability to influence business critical decisions and to formulate positive internal and external relationships. Works effectively on own initiative with the organisation and time management required to complete assignments on time and to the required quality standard. Enjoys being part of, as well as leading, a successful and productive audit team and thrives in highly pressurised and challenging working environments.

CAREER SUMMARY

2001–date   Accent on Accounting
                   Manager – Internal Audit Services

- Commencing employment as an Associate on a graduate training scheme working in external audit before gaining promotion through Senior Associate to Manager in internal audit
- Responsible for a number of key clients including Bunny Bros

Responsibilities and Achievements (Bunny Bros)

- Managing internal business process and licensee audit reviews for Bunny Home Video Entertainment as part of a global co-source contract across Asia Pacific, Europe and Middle East
- Completing Sarbanes Oxley reviews in the UK, France, Germany, Japan and Canada to facilitate full regulatory compliance
- Performance managing up to four UK and overseas based team members including setting objectives, providing coaching and work programmes, and contributing to their continuing professional development
- Ensuring accuracy and attention to detail when drafting internal audit reports, comprising information on issues, risks and innovative control recommendations
- Personally responsible for identifying claims in favour of Bunny Bros. totalling $1.1 million against all five licensees audits with two instances enabling the recovery of the audit fee
- Designing and implementing a strategy for long-term IT development within the business to enable the establishment of an e-commerce offering
- Producing budgets and long-term forecasts for subsequent presentation to the Banks
- Successfully increasing product lines by 300% while also reducing overall stockholding value by 25%
- Additionally driving down staff fixed costs by 20%

Responsibilities and Achievements (other clients)

- Managing internal audit plans for Computerserve plc, Neston plc and Express Train Group across EMEA and Asia Pacific involving extensive reporting to Partner and Directors and each respective Head of Internal Audit with excellent feedback received from each client

Page 1 of 2

CAREER SUMMARY cont.

- Negotiating and securing a £25 million group distribution contract resulting in a 10% reduction in overall distribution costs
- Driving down packaging costs by 28% as a result of initiating a reverse auctioning programme
- Creating and implementing a stock disposal programme, linked to catalogue printing, resulting in savings of £800,000 over two years
- Playing a lead role in the seamless completion of a £1.7 million office development and relocation project
- Redesigning the distributor commission package resulting in £500,000 savings per annum
- Introducing a new credit control system to enable a reduction in bad debts from 2.5% of turnover to just 0.8%
- Making a significant personal contribution to an overall growth in turnover from £20 million to £80 million in six years

General Achievements
- Initiating and concluding successful negotiations with Irish authorities to achieve a 50% reduction in output VAT
- Playing a pivotal role as Counselling Manager for five members of staff tasked with providing objective career guidance and assessing annual performance

EDUCATION AND QUALIFICATIONS

ACA: Institute of Chartered Accountants of Scotland (2004)
BSc (Hons): Business Economics – 2:1 (2001)
4 A Levels: Economics, French, German and General Studies (1998)
11 GCSEs: Including Business Studies, English and Mathematics (1996)

PROFESSIONAL DEVELOPMENT

- The Accent on Accounting Business Diploma (ongoing)
- Sarbanes Oxley Training and Expertise
- Six Sigma Orientation and Methodology Training

PROFESSIONAL MEMBERSHIPS

Associate Member: Institute of Cost & Executive Accountants (ACEA)

FURTHER SKILLS

IT Proficiency: Word, Excel, PowerPoint, MyClient, Aura, TeamMate and SAP
Languages: Intermediate French, German and Hindi; Basic Italian

INTERESTS AND ACTIVITIES

Currently include: Tennis, Snooker and Film/Cinema (especially Hitchcock)

REFERENCES ARE AVAILABLE ON REQUEST

ADMINISTRATION

SUSAN FARRER

1 Any Road, Anytown AN1 1CV
Telephone: 01632 960 551
Mobile: 07700 900 481
Fax: 01632 960 656
Email: susanfarrer@example.com

PROFESSIONAL PROFILE

A resourceful, hard-working and dedicated individual with outstanding administrative and organisational skills and the proven ability to develop and implement effective new systems and procedures. Possesses excellent IT skills with advanced knowledge of MS Office, is quick to grasp new ideas and concepts and always keen to develop new skills and expertise. Able to work well both independently and as part of a productive team, demonstrating the motivation and multi-tasking abilities required to meet demanding deadlines while maintaining the highest of standards. Articulate and proactive, combines a professional and confident approach with excellent interpersonal skills and can communicate concisely at all levels.

CAREER SUMMARY

2006–date   **Business Improvement Project Coordinator, Luton Ltd, London**

- Working as PA to the Programme Director with responsibility for developing, implementing and monitoring efficient office activities in addition to managing all correspondence
- Undertaking diary and event management and making travel arrangements as well as organising meetings with associated catering and accommodation
- Providing effective secretarial support and managing holiday requests and absence due to sickness for the project team and overseeing the office facilities
- Responsible as Project Coordinator for delivering a number of systems enhancements within the business improvement programme
- Consulting with staff at all levels to identify policy and best practice requirements as well as managing the Policy & Best Practice intranet site
- Making key contributions to the management of the communication plan while monitoring and updating programme plans on a wider basis
- Liaising with individual project teams to ensure the delivery of objectives while tracking the overall project progress and deliverables
- Preparing comprehensive consolidated project status and performance reports for the OpEx team

2005–2006   **PA/Office Manager, Leonardo plc, Godalming**

- Undertaking PA duties including diary management for the IT Director in addition to managing team expenses, diaries and schedules and the IT budget
- Coordinating travel and accommodation arrangements as well as managing meeting schedules and organising lunches and refreshments
- Creating a range of documentation including presentations, correspondence, memos and reports as well as taking minutes when required, and providing secretarial support for the team and management
- Carrying out IT procurement activities, monitoring third-party suppliers to ensure consistently good value as well as maintaining the IT standard catalogue
- Overseeing the smooth operation of the procurement process, managing work queues and evaluating performance tracking activities
- Compiling reports highlighting costs of products and services as well as preparing data for forecasting and budgeting
- Undertaking office management activities with responsibility for stationery, equipment and company mobile phones as well as organising company and rental vehicles
- Keeping accurate records of holiday and absence in addition to establishing data tracking systems and developing efficient office procedures

Page 1 of 2

CAREER SUMMARY cont.

2003–2005   **Sales and Training Coordinator, Simon Says Leisure, Woking**

- Working in a sales analyst role, preparing daily and monthly spreadsheets on behalf of the sales team and creating sales and performance graphs, sales and marketing presentations
- Maintaining the sales database as well as producing business reports on sales and income from membership joining fees and reconciling monthly commissions and quarterly bonuses
- Coordinating training activities, managing an online training diary and organising training events as well as preparing training packs and issuing joining instructions
- Delivering administrative support in sales and marketing as well as collating the training report on a monthly basis and organising accommodation, travel and refreshments as required

2000–2003   **Business Support Executive, Graphic Office Supplies, Guildford**

- Developing and delivering the online ordering system and training internal staff in its use in addition to providing administration of online accounts and the back-office system
- Demonstrating the online system to customers before closing sales, following up with system training as required
- Compiling online tutorials and training packs as well as providing full helpdesk support for the system

1998–2000   **PA/Marketing Coordinator, Anarchy Ltd, Winchester**

- Providing comprehensive PA support for the Sales and Marketing Director in addition to managing sales budgets and expenses and undertaking secretarial duties for the sales and marketing team
- Coordinating exhibitions, conferences and seminars in addition to organising mail shots and sourcing promotional items, liaising effectively with a range of suppliers and agencies
- Producing sales and marketing presentations as well as maintaining the database and delivering training as required

EDUCATION AND QUALIFICATIONS

ECDL	European Computer Driving Licence
NVQ2	Customer Services
5 GCSEs	Including English and Mathematics

FURTHER SKILLS

IT proficiency	MS Office, MS Project and SPSS
Languages	Intermediate Spanish

OTHER DETAILS

Driving licence	Full/Clean
Interests include	Hockey (captained Luton 2nd Eleven), Yoga and Violin

REFERENCES ARE AVAILABLE ON REQUEST

JAMES ROWE

1 Any Road, Anytown AN1 1CV
Telephone: 01632 960 791 (Home); 07700 900 214 (Mobile)
Email: jamesrowe@example.com

PROFESSIONAL PROFILE

An extremely conscientious, authoritative and dedicated individual, who enjoys the demands of high levels of accuracy and concentration, and flourishes with increased responsibilities. Quick and keen to learn, is diligent and meticulous, thrives in a demanding environment and relishes a technical challenge. Naturally self-motivated with lots of energy and enthusiasm, works well on own initiative and performs effectively under pressure. Personable and assured, possesses excellent interpersonal skills, can communicate concisely at all levels, and is a strong team builder and a natural leader, able to encourage disparate personalities to work in a team structure.

OBJECTIVE

Now looking for a new and challenging position, one that will make best use of current skills and experience and enable further personal and professional development towards the role of Production Supervisor.

CAREER SUMMARY

1995–date   ***Production Section Leader, John Velux Home Appliances, London***

- Initially starting as a programmer and setter of Bridgeport CNC machines, using both Fanuc and Heidenhain controls
- Gaining promotion to Production Section Leader of Aluminium Production
- Undertaking full accountability to meet the production schedule
- Successfully supervising and motivating 15 members of staff, delegating jobs and prioritising a production plan to achieve production targets and maintain all quality standards to ISO 9000
- Training all staff to high standards, encouraging precise tooling manufacture and facilitating the production of quality components
- Ordering tooling and assisting in the design and manufacture of production jigs and fixtures
- Implementing production efficiency and ensuring all personnel work to extremely high standards of health and safety
- Undertaking responsibilities of Qualified First Aider, Fire Marshall, Health and Safety Representative and Pensions committee member

Key Achievements:

- 1998: completed a quality report, focusing on scrap and rejected parts
- Implemented changes reducing scrap reducing by 17%
- 1999: reduced CNC production cost by incorporating ancillary forming and de-burring operations into machine cycle time with an annual saving of £11,500
- 2002: reduced production costs through tooling modification, by reducing the amount of operations when fabricating cooker door trims and saving an annual £8,300
- 2007: reduced costs of sub-contractor anodising by using an alternative method of finishing and lacquering components
- Detailed to go to Germany to purchase an appropriate machine and complete trials, bought a £40,000 machine which repaid its cost within 12 months
- Achieved 13 years of 100% attendance at work

Page 1 of 2

CAREER SUMMARY cont'd.

1976–1995   *Machinist Setter-Operator, Lockheed Precision Aviation (APPH), Slough*

- Undertaking a 4-year indentured apprenticeship in Mechanical Engineering with the company, working on lathes, milling, grinding machines and aircraft undercarriage assembly
- Gaining promotion to setter operator on conventional vertical and horizontal milling machines and lathes
- Gaining further promotion as setter operator on CNC milling machines (Mycente, Toyoda, Millwaukee, & Ajax) and CNC lathes (Okuma, Dean Smith and Grace)
- Achieving all production targets and ensuring the dimensional accuracy of components
- Completing all quality procedures to ISO 9000 standards

Key Achievements:
- Achieved City and Guild qualifications in Engineering 1,2,3,4
- Edited programmes and modified tooling to improve production efficiency

EDUCATION AND QUALIFICATIONS

City & Guilds:	Auto Cad Mechanical Design, Pass (2001)
NVQ:	Engineering CNC Machining, Pass (1996)
City & Guilds:	Mechanical Engineering, Credit (1980)
6 O Levels:	Including English & Mathematics (1976)

FURTHER SKILLS

I.T. Proficiency:	Word, Excel, Lotus Notes, Internet and Email
Languages:	Basic French, German and Italian

PERSONAL DETAILS

Nationality:	British
Driving Licence:	Full/Clean
Health:	Excellent; non-smoker
Other Details:	Qualified First Aider and Fire Marshall

INTERESTS AND ACTIVITIES

Currently include: Swimming, Tennis, Soccer, Cycling, Theatre, Art Galleries and Museums

REFERENCES ARE AVAILABLE ON REQUEST

GEORGE BUCHANAN

1 Any Road, Anytown AN1 1CV
Telephone: 01632 960 575 (Home); 07700 900 183 (Mobile)
Email: georgebuchanan@example.com

PROFESSIONAL PROFILE

An experienced and highly motivated business professional, with a proven record of success in both the travel and property industries, with a wealth of transferable skills, including outstanding interpersonal and staff management abilities. A capable organiser, quick to grasp – and make good use of – new ideas and information, and reliable and conscientious in all he takes on. Enjoys leading, motivating and being part of a productive team; equally comfortable working on own initiative. Possesses exemplary planning skills and accustomed to operating under considerable pressure, remaining calm and effective and prioritising wisely.

OBJECTIVE

Now looking for a challenging new position, one which will make good use of existing skills and experience while enabling further personal and professional development – ideally within account or event management, and connected to food or the hospitality industry.

CAREER SUMMARY

2006–present   *Owner/Director, Munch, Haywards Heath*

- Starting up and developing a highly successful business supplying fruit and vegetables to various public sector institutions
- Researching and preparing tenders; winning valuable contracts – for instance, with Leeds and Nottingham City Councils
- Dealing with all aspects of client relations and sales management, together with detailed financial control and reporting
- Managing two full-time staff and directing and monitoring the contracted-out packaging and delivery service

Key achievements

- Swiftly building turnover over three years from zero to an annual contract value of £1.5 million
- Winning – against considerable competition – a 12-month extension of the substantial Leeds contract

2002–2006   *Business Liaison Manager, Rural Enterprises, Slough*

- Assisting with post-Foot & Mouth rural business development – visiting a wide variety of enterprises and drawing on business experience to advise on marketing and management
- Initiating, planning and managing a number of well-attended locally-orientated promotional events and exhibitions

Key achievement

- Organising and overseeing all aspects of a lively three-day food festival, with 10,000 visitors

CAREER SUMMARY cont.

1998–2002   *General Manager/Director, The Scaynes Hill Hotel, Coniston Cold*

- Playing a key role in the building plans, fitting out and launch of a brand-new, 40-bedroom hotel on the edge of the Yorkshire Dales
- Responsible for recruiting and training the front-of-house team, establishing high standards of customer service and leading by example
- Dealing very capably with the crucial areas of PR, sales and marketing, and subsequently delivering 60% occupancy within 12 months of opening

Key achievement

- Winning Yorkshire Tourist Board and National CATEY 'Best Newcomer' awards

1990–1998   *Area Sales Manager, Register International Hotels*

- Heading a team of four Divisional Sales Managers and responsible for meeting the regional and national sales targets for a predominantly four-star hotel group
- Managing and successfully retaining the group's key accounts, with clients from government, banking and various agencies

EDUCATION AND QUALIFICATIONS

6 O Levels: Including English and Mathematics, all A–C (1983)

FURTHER SKILLS

IT Proficiency: MS Word, Excel, PowerPoint, Publisher and Access

PERSONAL DETAILS

Driving Licence: Full/Clean
Health: Excellent; non-smoker

INTERESTS AND ACTIVITIES

Currently include: Riding, going to the gym and football and creative writing

REFERENCES ARE AVAILABLE ON REQUEST

Christopher Cooper

address: **1 Any Road, Anytown AN1 1CV**
telephone: **01632 960 939**
mobile: **07700 900 232**
email: **christophercooper@example.com**

Professional profile

A dynamic senior manager with extensive procurement operations and project management experience within the retail sector. A competent strategist capable of developing innovative plans and activities designed to facilitate competitive growth and competitive superiority. Possesses excellent interpersonal, communication and negotiation skills, the ability to influence decisions and to develop positive relationships both internally and externally. Enjoys being part of, as well as managing, motivating, training and developing, a successful and productive team and thrives in highly pressurised and challenging working environments.

Career summary

2004–date   **J SAINSBURY PLC**

2008–date   **Senior Project Manager – International Buying Office**
- Creating and implementing an innovative strategy to facilitate the seamless integration of Turkey and Asia into IBO procurement
- Additionally responsible for the development of a key strategy for the Global Direct Sourcing function

2008   **Senior Buying Manager – Added Value Foods**
- Fully accountable for the Beers, Ales and Cider category with £711 million sales delivered across the UK and ROI on brands and own brand products
- Providing management and support to a dedicated buying and marketing team and motivating them towards the achievement of objectives
- Successfully streamlining processes whilst creating a buying scale by leveraging the international business
- Proactively managing increasing challenges including rising costs of commodities, duty and energy to enable J Sainsbury to outperform the market and retain market share

Key Achievements
- Successfully overachieving budgeted sales by 12% (£25 million) whilst negotiating an additional £12 million in business plan support

2004–2008   **Head of Category – Produce Group Sourcing**
- Personally responsible for the creation and implementation of a Produce Central Buying Process to leverage economy of scale for J Sainsbury Group and facilitate subsequent cost savings
- Managing day to day operations within Group Sourced Fresh Produce Category (vegetables, salads and horticulture) with responsibility for strategic growth and development
- Responsible for €208 million sales across the Group with a team of Buyers and Buying Managers based in UK, Ireland, Slovakia, Czech Republic, Hungary and Poland
- Delivering increased product quality and reduced costs in accordance with customer expectations as a direct result of developing capability within the team and the supply base

Key Achievements
- Receiving an award from Sainsbury's Main Board for delivering group savings of £20 million in the first year whilst simultaneously overachieving the savings budget by £800,000
- Consolidating and establishing fresh hubs in Czech Republic, Slovakia, Poland and Hungary to leverage economy of scale
- Leading on the implementation of a new buying structure, involving substantial operational change, new processes and systems to enable a move towards a Group Procurement Strategy and the implementation of best practices
- Playing a pivotal role as a senior member of a leadership team tasked with creating and expanding a multi-national produce buying team in the UK with achievements including delivering 60% of produce and horticulture procurement in CE and 5.5% of produce procurement in UK
- Introducing an innovative new range of cut flowers in CE with an annual budget of €20 million delivering 25% margin
- Establishing direct procurement from growers on Indian and Thai cut flowers to facilitate the delivery of the direct sourcing strategy

Career summary cont.

2003–2004 **UNITED WORLD COMMUNICATIONS, NAIROBI, KENYA**
Owner / Executive Director
- Establishing and managing a communications centre in Nairobi to provide unique communications options for the general and expatriate business community to enable NGOs and Missions to securely transact the financial aspects of their organisations

1997–2003 **TESCO UK LTD**
Head of Fresh Produce Procurement UK & ROI
- Commencing employment in a retail management and store expansion capacity before progressing through to Head of Produce responsible for seasonal non-food buying for UK and ROI
- Managing departmental operations covering 400 stores and 7 regional distribution centres with full accountability for 13% of company sales, £90 million annual turnover and profit margins in excess of 40%

Key Achievements
- Successfully doubling sales participation from 6.5% to 13% whilst driving a strong annual like for like of 15% and overall growth of 35% over 3 years
- Establishing a successful 7 days fresh cut flower business delivering 500% growth in the first year

1995–1996 **REGAL MOVING & STORAGE INC, NEW YORK, USA**
Director

1992–1994 **REPAKS TRANSPORTE GESMBHH, VIENNA, AUSTRIA**
Managing Director / Owner

1990–1992 **UN DISENGAGEMENT OBSERVER FORCES, DAMASCUS, SYRIA**
Military Police

Formal qualifications

Leadership Development Programme (2009)
- Business Leaders of Today
- Create the Vision & the Need for Change
- Sell & Communicate with Impact
- Gain Commitment & Engage Team
- Business Plan

Professional training

- Negotiation Skills
- Ethical Buying
- Advanced Negotiation Skills
- Situational Leadership
- Range Management
- Competition Act
- Coaching & Feedback
- Performance Management

Other details

Languages	Fluent German
IT proficiency	Word, Excel, PowerPoint and GMIS
Driving licence	Full/Clean
Interests include	Swimming, Cycling, Triathlons and Art (Painting)

References are available on request

Page 2 of 2

NATALIE SHAH

1 Any Road, Anytown AN1 1CV
Telephone: 01632 960 941; Mobile: 07700 900 935; Fax: 01632 960 316
Email: natalieshah@example.com

PROFESSIONAL PROFILE

> *A versatile and results-oriented professional who specialises in sourcing and buying products from UK and overseas markets requiring strong supplier relationships*

> *Familiar with all aspects of the consumer electronics market with particular emphasis on buying, marketing and e-commerce*

> *Possesses excellent interpersonal skills and the ability to communicate and negotiate concisely and articulately at all levels*

> *Attentive to detail with a practical approach to problem solving and the organisation required to ensure that deadlines, budgets and objectives are achieved*

> *Enjoys being part of a successful and productive team and thrives in highly pressurised and challenging working environments*

OBJECTIVE

Currently looking for a new and challenging position within the corporate sector, one which will make best use of existing skills and experience acquired in privately owned companies while enabling further personal and professional development.

CAREER SUMMARY

2005–date   FAR EAST MANAGER, *ABC Group LTD*

- Headhunted by the Chairman of the small family company specialising in the wholesale of consumer electronics products in the UK
- Tasked with the sole running and development of the company's interest in the China market, importing health food supplements, with full P&L and stockholding accountability
- Successfully increasing gross profits by 100% in the first full year with the business
- Driving sales into the UK health food market and achieving new sales of more than £1 million with projections for the following year of £3 million
- Cold calling prospective new customers and establishing a credit rating for them as well as sourcing products and negotiating prices with China
- Liaising extensively with UK customers to agree product specifications, sale prices and lead times
- Responsible for ensuring the accurate completion of associated paperwork including import documentation, which required liaising with Freight Forwarders and Port Health, with full accountability for the safe delivery of customer orders
- Travelling extensively to China to meet with new suppliers and to assess potential new products
- Actively involved in planning and organising the company's participation in a Health Food national event in September 2007

CAREER SUMMARY cont.

1985–2005   MANAGING DIRECTOR, *Sound & Vision Ltd*

- Commencing employment in the retail outlet before gaining a series of promotions culminating in the role of Managing Director for this privately owned company
- Negotiating terms and setting prices of consumer electronic and white goods product categories while maintaining awareness of budgetary constraints
- Playing a pivotal role in the launch and implementation of an e-commerce site, www.unbeatable.co.uk
- Interviewing, recruiting, training and mentoring new buyers into the business
- Setting budgets and forecasting sales whilst maintaining full P&L accountability
- Analysing buying trends and utilising this for the purposes of determining stock holding
- Creating and executing highly successful buying and sales promotions
- Responsible for a stock holding valued at up to £5 million and playing a key role in both in-store and online promotional activities
- Utilising strong skills in communication and negotiation to build mutually beneficial relationships with suppliers
- Establishing and developing concessions within the London stores Harrods and Selfridges

1982–1985   CLERK/CASHIER, *National Westminster Bank*

EDUCATION AND QUALIFICATIONS

9 O Levels   Including English and Mathematics

FURTHER SKILLS

IT Proficiency   Word, Excel, PowerPoint, Internet and Email
Languages   Basic French

PERSONAL DETAILS

Driving Licence   Full/Clean
Health   Excellent; non-smoker

INTERESTS AND ACTIVITIES

Include   Running, Keeping Fit and Cooking

REFERENCES ARE AVAILABLE ON REQUEST

RACHEL GRIFFITHS

1 Any Road, Anytown AN1 1CV
Telephone: 01632 960 898 (Home); 07700 900 623 (Mobile)
Email: rachelgriffiths@example.com

PROFESSIONAL PROFILE

A positive and professional retail and service manager who is passionate about delivering exceptional customer service standards while ensuring the achievement of demanding targets and corporate objectives. With a proven track record of achieving success in merchandising, driving sales, promoting brands and increasing turnover. A motivational and inspirational manager capable of coaching and empowering individuals to fulfil their potential as well as make a significant contribution to the business. Consistently demonstrates insight and shrewd judgement with the ability to devise innovative solutions to problems.

EDUCATION AND QUALIFICATIONS

CPC: Unit 1: Financial Management, Health & Safety Contract Law, Wakefield College (2009)
Examinations for Units 2 and 3 scheduled for 2010 will result in full Certificate of Professional Competence

CLAIT: OCR Level, Selby College (1996)

CAREER SUMMARY

1995–date *Group Manager, Adams Company Shops, Castleford*

- Responsible for managing two Adams staff shops serving staff, retired staff and contractors based at Castleford and at Halifax with full responsibility for all aspects of store management including staffing, premises, stock control, shrinkage, customer service and merchandising.
- Accountable for leading a team of 2 full-time one supervisor and 4 part-time staff to achieve sales and drive brand awareness among new and existing clients
- Recruiting, supervising, leading and motivating staff by maintaining excellent communication channels, conducting appraisals and ensuring they have the skills and tools to do their individual jobs effectively
- Conducting 6 weekly meetings with clients to review the status of their accounts and develop future strategic and operational plans
- Motivating and leading staff to exceed team targets and KPIs covering sales, customer satisfaction, training and budget control
- Controlling stock levels with due regard for procurement, shrinkage and cashflow
- Monitoring training and development for staff, analysing training needs, making recommendations for solutions and maintaining records
- Conducting audits to ensure stores comply with all regulatory requirements including Health & Safety, COSHH, risk assessment and finance
- Accountable for all financial transactions within the group including banking and agreeing/paying salaries
- Developing and implementing improved procedures and processes to ensure better and more consistent service throughout the stores
- Promoted to Manager in 2002 and Group Manager in 2004 as a result of outstanding performance and appraisal reviews

Page 1 of 2

CAREER SUMMARY cont.

1991–1995   *Store Manager, J&I Store, Knottingley*

- Fully accountable for all aspects of running a convenience store including managing the premises, security and housekeeping as well as ensuring compliance with all regulatory and legal guidelines, procedures and requirements
- Recruiting, motivating and supervising full-time and part-time staff, planning rotas and providing training, coaching and support to ensure they fulfil their potential and contribute effectively to the business
- Successfully devising and implementing a Customer Service Enhancement Programme, ensuring the whole team provide outstanding levels of service at all times and dealing personally with any customer complaints or problems
- Creatively planning promotions and implementing programmes to maximise merchandising opportunities and thus increase sales
- Controlling all store budgets and providing management information about sales, margins, forecasts, expenditure and local promotional or product opportunities
- Selected through merit to carry out the duties of the Area Manager's role during maternity leave absence

1974–1991   *Receptionist, A B Jones, Castleford*

- Appointed as a check-out operator and rapidly promoted to Receptionist
- Responsible for greeting all visitors and taking all in-bound calls with professionalism and sincerity
- Providing administrative support to colleagues by organising meetings, dealing with post, managing the file archiving programme and carrying out ad-hoc tasks as required
- Acting as the first point of contact for customer complaints and returns, and dealing with them if possible or escalating to an appropriate colleague

IT PROFICIENCY

- Nexus, EPOS, Word, Excel and PowerPoint

PERSONAL DETAILS

Driving Licence: Full/Clean
Health: Excellent; non-smoker

INTERESTS AND ACTIVITIES

Currently include: DIY, cooking, reading and hiking

REFERENCES ARE AVAILABLE ON REQUEST

PATRICIA HEPWORTH

1 Any Road, Anytown AN1 1CV
Telephone: 01632 960 739 (Home); 07700 900 709 (Mobile)
Email: patriciahepworth@example.com

Professional Profile

A dedicated and results-driven senior manager with a highly successful background in the achievement of profitable business growth through the creation and execution of successful sales and marketing strategies. Experienced in working with leading brands in the competitive retail and automotive industries with the primary focus on exceeding expectations for customer service delivery while ensuring optimum brand impact. Possesses excellent interpersonal, communication and negotiation skills and the ability to develop and maintain mutually beneficial internal and external relationships. Enjoys being part of, as well as managing, motivating and training, a successful and productive team, and thrives in highly pressurised and challenging working environments.

Career Summary

2005–2009 **TYRES UK LTD**
Freelance Consultant/Interim Network Development Manager

- Project managing the redevelopment of the retail sales strategy across the UK market with the ultimate aim of facilitating business performance improvements
- Successfully developing multi-channel solutions including instigating a new HiQ Fast Fit Franchise proposition
- Playing a pivotal role in the design and development of a class-leading B2C eBusiness website
- Working in close conjunction with external professionals to create and implement a retail network representation plan
- Actively involved in developing a new retail store concept and in redrafting all contractual agreements and process/procedure manuals
- Coordinating the pitch and scoping process for the selection of a staff training and development academy

1999–2005 **BDW GROUP**
2005–2005 **Managing Director, BDW Contact Ltd**

- Fully accountable for the establishment and management of a new business arm specialising in the provision of telemarketing services requiring the development of an independent customer base
- Collaborating with professionals and third parties to set up the infrastructure for the company and coordinating the recruitment, selection and training of 15 members of staff
- Planning and organising a highly successful launch programme and driving the business forward to break-even three months ahead of projections
- Introducing a range of B2B and B2C services and facilitating the provision of 24-hour service by business partnership in conjunction with an external agency

2000–2004 **Operations Director**

- Providing management and support to up to 68 members of staff and motivating them towards the achievement of optimum service delivery standards to facilitate customer satisfaction and maximum revenue generation
- Maintaining full profit and loss accountability up to £5 million while achieving a year-on-year growth in revenue of more than 10%
- Initiating half yearly service reviews with major blue chip, retail clients and formalising account planning to ensure best practice resulting directly in recognition for excellence in customer surveys
- Developing and implementing new billing and forecasting systems which significantly improved overall efficiency
- Enabling a 5% increase in actual gross margin in 1 year through the implementation of a staff incentive scheme

Career Summary cont.

1999–2000   Account Director

- Working in close conjunction with key client representatives to develop marketing strategies and point-of-sale materials on behalf of retail partners
- Negotiating and securing £120,000 in bespoke systems development revenue and playing a key role in increasing monthly revenue from £12,000 to £100,000

1996–1999   WORDS PICTURES SOUNDS
Managing Director

- Setting up and developing a full service design agency from the initial business planning, financial forecasting and business strategy development through to building and retaining the customer base
- Successfully securing and effectively managing contracts with leading brands including Audi, One 2 One and Cadbury for the provision of a range of creative services including media creative, brochure design, corporate identity and hard point of sale
- Achieving approved supplied status with Audi and One 2 One and delivering sustained income growth with the turnover increasing from £75,000 in 1996 to £750,000 in 1999

1983–1996   VAG (UK) LTD
Audi A8 Project Manager

- Commencing employment as a Trainee Field Sales Manager on behalf of the sole importers of Volkswagen and Audi vehicles and parts into the UK
- Gaining a series of promotions through various product, marketing, operations and advertising management positions, both head office and field based
- Ultimately undertaking the head office role of Audi A8 Project Manager tasked with the development and promotion of the brand and the vehicle within the luxury market with a total spend of £1.5 million

Education and Qualifications

4 A Levels   Mathematics, Economics, History and General Studies
8 O Levels   Including English and Mathematics

Professional Development

- Management Development Programme
- Marketing Management
- Presentation Skills
- Finance for Non-financial Managers

- Effective Man Management
- Appraisal Training
- Team Building
- Creativity Training

IT Skills

- Word, Excel, Access, PowerPoint, Internet and Email

Personal Details

Driving Licence   Full/Clean
Health   Excellent; non-smoker
Interests   Squash, Golf, Reading (current affairs), Theatre and Cuisine

References Are Available On Request

SALES

Tony Crockford

1 Any Road, Anytown AN1 1CV
Telephone: 07700 900 218
Email: tonycrockford@example.com

PROFESSIONAL PROFILE

A dynamic and results-driven professional with a highly successful background in sales, account management and new business development. Committed to achieving and exceeding demanding targets and business objectives while remaining focused on providing an exceptional standard of service to international and UK clients. Possesses excellent interpersonal, communication and negotiation skills, the ability to influence decisions and to develop positive internal and external relationships. Enjoys being part of, as well as managing and motivating, a successful and productive team and thrives in highly pressurised and challenging working environments.

CAREER SUMMARY

2008–date   VAUCAN-HAMSTER LTD, Sales Associate

- Playing a key role as a Sales Associate within the newly established Marketing Business Development Department set up as a business development project to assist in generating opportunities across four practice verticals: general enterprise, industrial, technical and consumer products
- Personally responsible for driving revenue growth across these verticals by collaborating with clients on the provision of consulting and training services according to their needs utilising a range of problem solving, project execution and business process improvement applications
- Actively involved in outbound calling to facilitate the identification and qualification of sales leads across all practices
- Planning and executing innovative campaigns, including direct mail, webcasts, catalogue distribution and thought leadership, to generate new sales leads in EMEA and NA regions
- Developing positive relationships with potential clients, establishing their business needs and developing solutions based around Vaucan-Hamster services
- Preparing and delivering successful pitches to director, senior and middle management level prospects
- Additionally responsible for preparing and presenting detailed campaign analysis and reports to practice leaders

Key Achievements

- Playing a key role in promoting cross practice value propositions for consulting engagements and executive training solutions to develop strategic and operational problem solving and decision making, project management and business process improvements for issue resolution
- Contributing directly to the new department delivering 98% of leads target/plan and 98% of revenue target/plan within the first year
- Personally responsible for bringing in new leads to the organisation with values ranging from £10,000 to £50,000
- Currently involved in developing partnership deals within strategically aligned markets and territories within the Middle East
- Utilising previous expertise in developing internal departmental processes to lead on the creation and re-design of departmental systems to standardise project execution and campaign management/analysis

2005–2008   MEGA MEDIA LTD, Sales Executive (temporary)

- Initially undertaking a telesales based role for the regional lifestyle publication tasked with selling all forms of advertising space from classified to display page
- Gaining rapid promotion, after just 2 months, to a field based role covering two SE territories/publications with full accountability for the complete sales cycle including presenting at field appointments and closing agreements
- Liaising directly with events editors and photographers to facilitate appropriate coverage of planned events

Key Achievements

- Achieving personal recognition as the top sales person in the company despite only being employed on a 6-month contract
- Facilitating a sales growth for the area by 27% and £184K during the first year

2002–2005   AMOUR DISTRIBUTION LTD, Head of International Sales

- Responsible for the account management of key sub-distribution partnerships involving regular sales and strategy meetings at director level and overseas business meetings and visits
- Providing comprehensive advice to clients on all aspects of retail marketing, press and radio promotions
- Generating sales and budget analysis reports to enable the communication of departmental sales progress and performance

Page 1 of 2

CAREER SUMMARY cont.

Key Achievements

- Enjoying considerable success in terms of delivering in excess of £3.5 million annual department budgets
- Achieving year-on-year sales increases having successfully forecasted and planned departmental budgets
- Piloting and managing the successful development of a CD sub-distribution network in key overseas territories including USA, Canada, Australia, Germany, Benelux, Spain and France and concluding negotiations to secure exclusive product agreements
- Playing a pivotal role in the development of new business within existing networks of Direct Europe and UK export accounts having brokered exclusive product deals and campaigns
- Winning the International Trade & Export Award 2005 from Watford & North West London Business Association

2000–2002   **RENAISSANCE DISTRIBUTION LTD, Import Singles Manager**

- Responsible for the management of the singles department within the busy music wholesale company
- Managing an extensive portfolio of UK retail accounts with key clients such as HMV, Virgin and Tower, including delivering presentations to buyers and providing a first point of contact for all singles based product enquiries
- Attending weekly field sales meetings with London based major chain accounts and working with them to discuss and resolve any issues that may arise
- Recruiting and managing the dedicated telesales team and providing them with comprehensive training and support as required

Key Achievements

- Consistently achieving monthly and annual sales targets and playing a key role in delivering 20% business growth
- Contributing directly to the company achieving preferred supplier status with key national accounts for the import of singles products

1997–2000   **VIRGIN LTD, Product Buyer**

- Fully accountable for purchasing all chart and non-chart eligible singles products whilst maintaining awareness of budgetary constraints, sales and stock targets
- Developing and maintaining mutually beneficial relationships across an extensive network of UK suppliers

EDUCATION AND QUALIFICATIONS

DipHE:	Popular Music Performance
Drumtech Diploma:	Drums and Percussion
8 GCSEs:	Including English and Mathematics

PROFESSIONAL TRAINING

- Project Management: PMI Accredited
- Lean Manufacturing/Lean Office
- Incident Mapping
- Problem Solving & Decision Making for Investigations and CAPAS

KEY IT SKILLS

- Word, Excel, PowerPoint, Salesforce, Internet and Email

PERSONAL DETAILS

Driving Licence:	Full/Clean
Health:	Excellent; non-smoker
Interests include:	Running, Swimming, Golf and Guitar playing

REFERENCES ARE AVAILABLE ON REQUEST

Page 2 of 2

James Catterall

1 Any Road, Anytown AN1 1CV
Telephone: 07700 900 826
Email: jamescatterall@example.com

PROFESSIONAL PROFILE

A highly experienced professional who effectively combines strong technical, problem-solving and planning capabilities to successfully deliver projects on time and on budget. Possesses excellent interpersonal skills and the ability to communicate professionally with clients, architects, suppliers and sub-contractors alike. Enjoys being part of, as well as managing and motivating, a successful and productive team and thrives in highly pressurised and challenging working environments.

CAREER SUMMARY

2003–date   **MOORSIDE CONSTRUCTION, NOTTINGHAM**
Site Manager

- Playing a pivotal role in the lifecycle management of a wide range of projects, ranging in scale and value, from the initial concept through to completion
- Providing management and support to all site personnel and developing and maintaining productive relationships with clients, architects and sub-contractors
- Monitoring and controlling all work activities with the primary focus on ensuring compliance with health and safety regulations
- Sourcing and recruiting sub-contractors and purchasing materials while maintaining awareness of budgetary constraints
- Working collaboratively to ensure that all projects are completed on time and within programme targets
- Producing and reviewing weekly and monthly progress reports and taking appropriate action to resolve any issues that are identified

Summary of Projects

- New build project of two luxury houses in Gerrard's Cross, Buckinghamshire (resale value £4 million)
- Refurbishment of 36 apartments in Nottingham City Centre (resale value £4.1 million)
- Modernisation of premises to accommodate glass company, Bridgwater (project costs £40,000)
- Preparing of sites for a construction phase including the demolition of existing buildings, Bridgwater
- High specification fit out of office units in Nottingham City Centre (project value for refurbishment £70,000)
- Development of several 4/5 bedroom luxury detached houses in Derbyshire (project value £900,000)
- Refurbishment of 4-bedroom bungalow in Derbyshire (refurbishment costs £30,000)
- Refurbishment of office premises in Surrey (costs £7,000)
- Fit out of 16 luxury apartments in Nottingham City Centre (resale value of £1.8 million)
- Development of 52 luxury retirement apartments in Plympton (resale value of £8.5 million)

2001–2003   **TONY JARVIS, TEIGNMOUTH**
Bricklayer / Chippies Mate

- Working both independently and alongside specific trades on a variety of new build and refurbishment projects with responsibility for the achievement of targets and compliance with health and safety legislation

2001   **PRIVATE CLIENT, PLYMOUTH**
General Builder

- Playing a key role in the modernisation and improvement of a 7-bedroom farm house in Oakhampton
- Undertaking a wide variety of tasks including installation of first-floor timbers, plastering, tiling and the formation of an extensive patio area

CAREER SUMMARY cont.

1999–2001 **PRIVATE CLIENT, FRANCE**
General Builder

- Working on the modernisation and improvement of various dwellings involving take-offs and materials ordering and planning the sequence of works

1997–1999 **BUDWEISER, GLASGOW**
Machine Operator / Maintenance Engineer

- Responsible for the safe operation of plant and machinery and for responding to any breakdowns that may arise

EDUCATION AND QUALIFICATIONS

NHBC NVQ: Site Manager Development Level IV (ongoing)
NVQ: Mechanical & Electrical Engineering Level II
Certificate: Agriculture
6 Standards: Including English and Mathematics

PROFESSIONAL TRAINING

- Construction Site Managers Safety Certificate
- Business/Construction Management Course
- Construction Certification Training
- First Aid at Work
- Fork Lift Certificate Class 1/2/3
- Manual Handling Certificate
- Abrasive Wheels Certificate
- Plastic Moulding Course

KEY IT SKILLS

- Word, Excel, Internet and Email

PERSONAL DETAILS

Driving Licence: Full/Clean
Health: Excellent; non-smoker
Other Details: Qualified First Aider

INTERESTS AND ACTIVITIES

Currently include: Gym Training, Paragliding, Off-road Motor Biking and Mountain Biking

REFERENCES ARE AVAILABLE ON REQUEST

RICKY WOOLF

1 Any Road, Anytown AN1 1CV
Telephone: 01632 960 898 (Home); 07700 900 138 (Mobile)
Email: rickywoolf@example.com

PROFESSIONAL PROFILE

A committed and proactive professional who specialises in the use of embedded design and programming techniques to develop creative and innovative robotic systems tailored towards specific project requirements. Quick to assimilate new ideas, concepts and cutting-edge technologies whilst demonstrating a logical and analytical approach to solving complex problems and issues. Able to work well on own initiative while demonstrating the organisation and prioritisation required to achieve tight deadlines and deliverables. A motivational and inspirational leader who enjoys being part of a successful and productive team, and thrives in highly pressurised and challenging working environments.

OBJECTIVE

Currently looking for a new and challenging position, one which will make best use of existing skills and experience while enabling further personal and professional development.

EDUCATION AND QUALIFICATIONS

MSc   Embedded Systems and Robotics – Distinction (2003)
Thesis: *Compact Motion Tracking System for Human Rehabilitation*
BSc   Computer Science with Robotics & Intelligent Machines – 2.1 (2002)
Thesis: *2D Mapping Mobile Robots in Unstructured Environments*
College Courses   Mathematics, Mechatronic Systems, Applied Dynamics and Electrical
Control Theory

KEY TECHNICAL SKILLS

- Assembler, Embedded C, C++, Visual MFC, Linux, Java, OpenGL, Handle-C and VHDL

CAREER SUMMARY

2005–date   *Mobile Robotics Ltd, London*
SENIOR RESEARCH ASSISTANT

- Playing a lead role in the research team tasked with developing a range of underwater robotic research vehicles, a £2.2 million project funded by the London Zoo
- Actively involved in the commercial aspects of the project to facilitate the achievement of demanding deadlines and deliverables, enabling the project to proceed to the next phase
- Providing a prompt and appropriate response to unforeseen mechanical and electrical design problems including making innovative decisions to prevent future repercussions
- Successfully developing a range of underwater robotic vehicles including both remote controlled and autonomous vehicles
- Additionally developing and testing materials, control and navigation systems to facilitate the achievement of operational functionality

CAREER SUMMARY cont.

2003–2005   **University of Exeter, Devon**
RESEARCH ASSISTANT

- Specifically responsible for the design and development of a low-cost, accurate, unobtrusive sensor to enable in-home, unaided rehabilitation on behalf of stroke victims
- Tasked with ensuring minimal hardware installation requirements within the patient's home environment requiring the team to overcome the obstacles associated with the use of camera tracking and body markers to enable the accurate mapping of limb movements
- Developing a wireless system using the Bluetooth protocol to minimise the problems usually associated with the weight of systems, the restriction of movement and visible wiring
- Overcoming the charging issues common with using very small batteries by designing a system that can be inductance charged at the end of each session

POSTGRADUATE TEACHING ASSISTANT

- Assisting with the delivery of laboratory sessions to undergraduates in the following subjects: Embedded Programming; C/C++ Programming; Electronic Hardware Design (PCB Design); Robotic Control Systems

1990–1998   **UVW Engineering Ltd, Cuckfield**
TECHNICAL ENGINEER

- Responsible for the repair and maintenance of agricultural vehicles including overhauling engines and transmission units and diagnosing and repairing faults

VOLUNTARY WORK

2005–date   **University of Cambridge/University of Oxford**
MACHINE CONSCIOUSNESS LABORATORY

- Actively involved in the resolution of design problems in the fields of electrical sensory feedback and mechanical systems within compliant anthropomimetic robotics

PERSONAL DETAILS

Driving Licence   Full/Clean
Health   Excellent; non-smoker

INTERESTS AND ACTIVITIES

Currently include   Fitness Training, Cooking and Astronomy
Other   Currently learning German

REFERENCES ARE AVAILABLE ON REQUEST

Page 2 of 2

Phil Brown

1 Any Road, Anytown AN1 1CV
Telephone: 07700 900 002
Email: philbrown@example.com

PROFESSIONAL PROFILE

A dedicated and enthusiastic CCVP accredited professional who specialises in project managing innovative voice and data solutions to improve system stability, functionality and efficiency. Quick to familiarise himself with the latest technologies and industry developments while demonstrating a logical and analytical approach to solving complex problems and issues. Possesses excellent interpersonal and communication skills and the ability to develop and maintain positive internal and external relationships. Enjoys being part of, as well as leading, a successful and productive team and thrives in highly pressurised and challenging working environments.

CAREER SUMMARY

2001–date   BANK OF QUEBEC, Senior LAN/WAN & Voice Technical Analyst

- Working as part of the Trading Services Group tasked with providing 1st, 2nd and 3rd line support to 200 users and 100 traders in London and 40 traders in 8 European offices
- Generally responsible for the maintenance and programming of the Nortel/Cisco data network including programming routing, MLT, SMLT, Trunks, VLANs, VLAN tagging and ACLs
- Diagnosing and resolving faults with the BT ITS Netrix dealerboard system, Nortel CS1000e VoIP and Nicelog call logging system
- Providing comprehensive support to end users of trading platforms including Bloomberg, Reuters, Orderboard and RDMS
- Additionally involved in providing Wintel support including AD, Server 2003, NAS, blade servers and blade workstations
- Developing and implementing procedures for new starters and leavers, and adding or deleting services in the bank

Key Projects and Achievements

- Playing a lead technical role in a major project to relocate to new offices including the implementation of new dealerboard/VoIP systems and a new Nortel/Cisco network
- Fully accountable for planning the move phases relating to the data and voice infrastructure for the new offices and working with external vendors to install and configure equipment
- Leading on the implementation of a new cabling/port database used to track all ports and connections in the infrastructure of the bank and producing procedures relating to moves/additions for audit purposes
- Taking appropriate action in response to audit results to facilitate improvements to the infrastructure network and voice systems and, as a result, achieving perfect scores from the audit team in 2004 and 2005
- Negotiating and securing a new maintenance contract for the voice/data systems resulting in substantial reductions in costs and a simultaneous improvement in SLA response times

2000–2001   NOKIA COMMUNICATIONS LTD, Senior Network Support Analyst

- Providing management and support to a team of eight 2nd and 3rd line support technicians tasked with the maintenance and fault diagnosis of the extensive Centrica voice network supporting 20,000 users and AXA network supporting 15,000 users
- Dialling into Mitel SX2000 and MD110 switches and collaborating with third-party suppliers to identify and rectify faults
- Meeting regularly with suppliers and liaising with third-party vendors with responsibility for escalating faults to SDMs and account managers for resolution
- Updating lines of business for priority faults and monitoring the team to ensure that issues are resolved in accordance with SLAs

Key Achievements

- Analysing procedures, escalation points and major faults and making subsequent recommendations to prevent the same problems from occurring

Page 1 of 2

CAREER SUMMARY cont.

1998–2000   EFG INFORMATION SYSTEMS, EFG Technician Level 6
- Working within a busy dealing room environment with responsibility for the support, installation and fault finding of EFG MX and EFG Tradenet sites
- Supporting 150 traders including performing backups, amending records, adding/ceasing lines and implementing dealerboard changes

1997–1998   EASTMAN INSURANCE SERVICES LTD, IT Communications Technician
- Providing 2nd line support for six Meridian and two ISDX networked switches involving the use of Eclipse to log all calls received
- Responsible for the network infrastructure and for undertaking some project management for Meridian upgrades and moves
- Utilising Memotec clusters, case smartmuxes and kilostreams for the installation and maintenance of the RS232 and X25 data network

EDUCATION AND QUALIFICATIONS

CCNA: Cisco Certified Network Associate
CCVP: Cisco Certified Voice Professional
BTEC: National Diploma in I.T. Applications

PROFESSIONAL TRAINING

- VoIP
- Project Management
- BT ITS Netrix
- HP Nas/Storage Mirroring
- Managing Windows Server 2003
- Implementing & Supporting XP
- Nortel Device Manager
- Nortel Networking
- Network+ N10-002

- MD 1000 Admin & Maintenance
- Telebusiness 200 Installation & Maintenance
- ISDN BRI/PRI Installation & Maintenance
- SX2000 Installation & Maintenance
- EFG MX
- Astro Data Communications/X25
- Wadsworth Cat 5 Installation
- BT Meridian Administrator

KEY TECHNICAL SKILLS

- Cisco IPT
- Nortel CS1000e IPT
- VoIP
- Nortel & Cisco LAN/WAN Networks
- BT ITS Netrix Dealerboards
- EFG MX/Tradenet Dealerboards
- Nicelog
- Windows Server 2003
- Windows XP

- Mitel SX2000
- Mitel Telebusiness 2000
- Meridian PBX
- Meridian ACD
- CAT5 Cabling
- HP Openview
- Tevista
- Bloomberg
- Reuters D3000

PERSONAL DETAILS

Driving Licence: Full/Clean
Health: Excellent; non-smoker
Interests include: Fishing, Motor Sports and Football

REFERENCES ARE AVAILABLE ON REQUEST

Martin Wardle

address: 1 Any Road, Anytown AN1 1CV
telephone: 01632 960 326
mobile: 07700 900 285
e-mail: martinwardle@example.com

Professional profile

An enthusiastic and professional Web Designer, who enjoys being part of, as well as leading, a successful and productive team. Quick to grasp new ideas and concepts, and to develop innovative and creative solutions to problems. Able to work well on own initiative and can demonstrate the high levels of motivation required to meet the tightest of deadlines. Even under significant pressure, possesses a strong ability to perform effectively.

Objective

Now looking to build on extensive range of technical skills within a suitably challenging role. Keen to achieve further professional development.

Key technical skills

Adobe PhotoShop	Macromedia Dreamweaver	QuarkXPress
Adobe Illustrator	Macromedia Flash	Strata Studio Pro (3D)
Adobe Premiere	Macromedia Director	FTP Programs
Adobe After Effects	Poser	Bryce 3D
Adobe Acrobat	QTVR	Microsoft Excel
Microsoft PowerPoint	Equilibrium	Media Cleaner Pro

Career summary

2006–date   **Webmaster, Graphics UK, London**
- Working within a major print design company, tasked with developing their fledgling Web Department
- Assessing initial set-up requirements and implementing hardware and software solutions accordingly
- Training the team in the use of QuarkXPress, Beyond Press Pro, PhotoShop, Dreamweaver, Media Cleaner Pro, QTVR and Adobe Premier
- Coordinating closely with Account Executives, actively soliciting new clients and nurturing existing client accounts, ensuring their needs and requirements were not only accommodated but surpassed
- Winning over many clients from larger companies, due to the extremely high standards of creative design work
- Training clients in subsequent website maintenance, particularly the use of Dreamweaver and its inbuilt FTP facility
- Initiating a company-wide changeover to a much faster ISP with enhanced technical support
- Clients include major blue chip companies such as the British Land Company and Millennium Diamonds as well as many high-profile government departments and agencies

Selected portfolio

www.website.com
www.onewithtext.com
www.onewithgraphics.com
www.personalwebsite.com

www.anotherwebsite.com
www.andanother.com
www.flashwebsite.com
www.onemoreexample.com

Education and qualifications

2003–2006   National Diploma in Graphic Design & Multimedia (First Class Honours)
Dublin Institute of Technology, Ireland

Key Modules: Web Design, Visual Communication, Multimedia, Print Design, Typography & Photography

Won the **Multimedia Student of the Year Award** and **Best Use of a Mac Award**.

Professional development

- Team Leadership (Management Training Centre, 2009)
- Presentation Skills (Management Training Centre, 2008)

Personal details

Driving Licence   Full/Clean
Health   Excellent; non-smoker
Languages   Fluent French & German

Interests and activities

Currently include   Photography, Theatre & Amateur Dramatics, Football and Golf

References are available on request

Colin Smith

1 Any Road, Anytown AN1 1CV
Telephone: 01632 960 452 (Home); 07700 900 973 (Mobile)
Email: colinsmith@example.com

PROFESSIONAL PROFILE

A disciplined and dedicated professional with an expert knowledge of logistics, inventory and supply chain management acquired during more than 20 years service with the Royal Air Force. Specialises in delivering improvements in performance and efficiency through the implementation of Lean and value-adding processes whilst remaining focused on achieving service excellence. Able to work effectively on own initiative with the organisation and prioritisation required to achieve tight deadlines and budgets. Possesses excellent interpersonal, communication and negotiation skills, and the ability to develop positive relationships both internally and externally. Enjoys being part of, as well as managing and developing, a successful and productive team and thrives in highly pressurised and challenging working environments.

OBJECTIVE

Currently looking for a new and challenging position in the civilian logistics arena, one that will make best use of existing skills and experience whilst enabling further personal and professional development.

EDUCATION AND QUALIFICATIONS

CILT: Advanced Diploma in Logistics & Transport Level 6 (ongoing)
Professional Diploma in Logistics & Transport (NVQ Level 5/Degree) (2008)
NVQ: Distribution Warehousing Operations Level 3
Warehousing Wholesaling Stores Level 2

AFFILIATIONS

- Chartered Institute of Logistics & Transport (MILT)
- Chartered Institute of Leadership & Management (MinstLM)
- European Logistics Association (ESLog)

KEY IT SKILLS

- Word, Excel, PowerPoint, Internet and Email

CAREER SUMMARY

1987–2009 **ROYAL AIR FORCE**

2006–2009 **Logistics Manager**
- Managing the procurement of all fuels, lubricants and associated aviation products utilising computerised Inventory Management Systems
- Playing a key role in the overall strategic direction of the department with the focus on achieving demanding KPIs and SLAs
- Working in close conjunction with external agencies to ensure that sufficient inventory levels are maintained in accordance with customer demands with total stock values in excess of £15 million
- Utilising Enterprise Resource Planning databases to maintain strict control over inventory levels and to ensure asset integrity

Key Achievement
- Spearheading the implementation of a Lean event within the department resulting in savings in inventory costs and labour hours by removing non-value adding activities from each work process

CAREER SUMMARY cont.

2003–2006   Logistics Manager – Search & Rescue (SAR)
- Senior Supply Representative and Logistics Specialist supporting Search & Rescue (SAR) operations across the eastern region of the UK whilst simultaneously fulfilling client's logistical requirements
- Responsible for ensuring that sufficient fuel levels are maintained within the supply depot in order to satisfy demand
- Maintaining optimum levels of aircraft inventory with a stock value in excess of £30 million and undertaking accounting procedures in accordance with National Audit Office policy
- Facilitating the timely expedition of aircraft critical assets for transportation and distribution throughout the UK and overseas
- Line managing other staff within the division including dealing with welfare issues and facilitating their career development
- Overseeing the testing of lifecycle products in conjunction with test laboratories and maintaining a first-in, first-out policy of unit stock

Key Achievement
- Developing and implementing a maintenance programme for an old bulk fuel storage depot to enable it to meet stringent quality, health & safety and petroleum standards

2000–2003   Direct Support Manager
- Playing a pivotal role as the primary interface between the RAF, British Aerospace and the Royal Saudi Air Force (RSAF) to ensure that procurement requests from the RSAF are fulfilled
- Periodically reviewing the activities of the prime contractor to ensure that performance levels are maintained in accordance with SLAs
- Liaising extensively between the three agencies to ensure a constant flow of information in order to meet and exceed KPIs
- Coordinating the timely expedition of high value inventory to overseas destinations in accordance with customer deadlines and requirements
- Controlling the sale and loan of high value equipment to the RSAF under the terms of the Al Yamamah government led project
- Participating in high level meetings to provide advice to respective agencies regarding all aspects of logistics and procurement

Key Achievement
- Successfully reducing aircraft on the ground demands for the client whilst simultaneously selling 2,000 assets to the client resulting in £2.5 million being recouped by the RAF

1991–2000   Logistician – Royal Air Force, Leeds

PERSONAL DETAILS

Driving Licence: Full/Clean
Health: Excellent; non-smoker
Interests include: Sports, Computers, Music and Siberian Huskies

REFERENCES ARE AVAILABLE ON REQUEST

PART 9

MY FIVE TOP TIPS TO MAKE YOUR CV STAND OUT

If you only had time to read one page of *The CV Book*, this is the page I would most like you to have taken the time to read. See it as a 'cheat sheet'. It encapsulates the most important principles that we have covered in the book. Make an effort to accommodate all these when writing your CV and you'll immediately be well above average.

1 Maximise readability

It is essential for your CV to be easy for the reader to scan quickly and effectively. You need to separate different sections and insert clear section headings. Avoid long paragraphs; use bullet pointing to break up text into more manageable 'bite-size' chunks. It should be eye-catching and uncluttered. Check vigilantly for spelling and grammatical errors.

2 Include a Professional Profile and Objective

These sections should summarise and emphasise your key attributes and your intended future career path. Your words must flow seamlessly – avoiding cliché and superfluous hyperbole.

3 Include Achievements where possible

If you can include an *Achievements* section then it can make an instant and dramatic difference to the power of your CV, enabling you to distinguish yourself from other candidates.

4 Keep your CV concise and to-the-point

Your CV should be informative – but also concise. In general, two A4 pages is a maximum. Too many CVs are quite simply too long. Only include information which will actually help to sell you. Recruiters don't want to waste time reading details irrelevant to your ability to fulfil the job role.

5 Target/tailor your CV

If possible, tailor your CV according to the specific vacancy for which you are applying. A carefully targeted CV can easily mean the difference between success and failure.

Conclusion

Writing a CV is not rocket science! Most of what I have outlined is reasonably simple to take on board and it's just a matter of putting in the necessary time and effort.

I do hope you have found *The CV Book* useful. Don't forget to visit the CV Centre's online forum to let us know how you get on:

http://www. ineedacv.co.uk/forum

You will also have the opportunity to make contact with me and my team directly.

GOOD LUCK!

Further reading and resources

Recommended Books

Borg, J. (2007) *Persuasion: The Art of Influencing People*, Prentice Hall Business Hall Life

Borg, J. (2008) *Body Language: 7 Easy Lessons to Master the Silent Language*, Prentice Hall Life

Bright, J. and Earl, J. (2008) *Brilliant CV*, 3rd Edition, Prentice Hall Business

Edenborough, R. (2009) *Brilliant Psychometric Tests*, Prentice Hall Business

Fagan, A. (2007) *Brilliant Job Hunting*, 2nd Edition, Prentice Hall Business

Faust, B. and Faust, M. (2006) *Pitch Yourself*, 2nd Edition, Prentice Hall Business

Hall, R. (2008) *The Secrets of Success at Work: 10 Steps to Accelerating Your Career*, Prentice Hall Business

Hodgson, S. (2007) *Brilliant Tactics to Pass Aptitude Tests*, 2nd Edition, Prentice Hall Business

Hodgson, S. (2008) *Brilliant Answers to Tough Interview Questions*, 3rd Edition, Prentice Hall Business

Innes, J. (2009) *Brilliant Cover Letters*, Prentice Hall Business

Innes, J. (2009) *The Interview Book*, Prentice Hall Business

Jay, R. (2008) *Brilliant Interview*, 2nd Edition, Prentice Hall Business

Johnson, S. (2007) *Brilliant Word 2007*, Prentice Hall Business

Perkins, G. (2007) *Killer CVs & Hidden Approaches*, 3rd Edition, Prentice Hall Business

Taylor, N. (2008) *Brilliant Business Writing*, Prentice Hall Business

Templar, R. (2002) *The Rules of Work: A Definitive Guide to Personal Success*, Prentice Hall Business

Yeung, R. (2008) *Confidence: The Art of Getting Whatever You Want*, Harlow: Prentice Hall Life

These titles are available from all major bookshops. You can also learn more about them and even place an order for a copy by visiting the following page on our website: **http://www.ineedacv.co.uk/recommendedbooks**

Online resources

I keep my list of online resources – online. That way I can keep it bang up-to-date at all times. Please access the following page for a wide range of useful links to job sites and other online resources.

http://www.ineedacv.co.uk/resources

Appendix A:
250 action verbs

Accomplished
Achieved
Acquired
Administered
Advised
Advocated
Analysed
Anticipated
Appointed
Appraised
Approved
Arbitrated
Arranged
Articulated
Assembled
Assessed
Assisted
Attained
Audited
Augmented
Authorised
Averted
Avoided
Balanced
Began
Bought
Briefed
Budgeted
Built
Calculated
Captured
Centralised
Changed

Clarified
Classified
Coached
Collated
Collected
Combined
Communicated
Completed
Composed
Compounded
Conceived
Conducted
Conserved
Consolidated
Constructed
Consulted
Contributed
Controlled
Converted
Convinced
Coordinated
Corrected
Corresponded
Counselled
Created
Criticised
Dealt
Debated
Decided
Decreased
Defined
Delegated
Delivered

Demonstrated
Designated
Designed
Detected
Determined
Developed
Devised
Diagnosed
Diminished
Directed
Discovered
Dispensed
Disproved
Distributed
Documented
Doubled
Dropped
Earned
Edited
Educated
Effected
Elected
Eliminated
Employed
Enabled
Encouraged
Enforced
Engineered
Enjoyed
Ensured
Established
Estimated
Evaluated

Examined	Led	Produced
Exceeded	Liaised	Profited
Executed	Liquidated	Programmed
Expanded	Located	Promoted
Expedited	Logged	Protected
Explained	Maintained	Proved
Explored	Managed	Provided
Extracted	Mapped	Published
Facilitated	Marketed	Purchased
Forecast	Maximised	Raised
Formed	Mediated	Ran
Formulated	Modernised	Rated
Fostered	Modified	Realised
Founded	Monitored	Received
Functioned	Motivated	Recognised
Gained	Named	Recommended
Galvanised	Navigated	Reconciled
Gathered	Negotiated	Recorded
Generated	Networked	Recruited
Guided	Observed	Redesigned
Handled	Obtained	Reduced
Heightened	Operated	Referred
Highlighted	Ordered	Regulated
Hired	Organised	Rejected
Identified	Originated	Related
Implemented	Oversaw	Rendered
Improved	Participated	Reorganised
Improvised	Perceived	Represented
Increased	Performed	Researched
Initiated	Pioneered	Resolved
Inspected	Placed	Restored
Inspired	Planned	Reviewed
Installed	Positioned	Revised
Instigated	Prepared	Revitalised
Instituted	Prescribed	Routed
Instructed	Presented	Saved
Interacted	Prevailed	Scheduled
Introduced	Prevented	Scrutinised
Invented	Prioritised	Selected
Investigated	Processed	Sent
Launched	Procured	Served

Settled
Shaped
Simplified
Sold
Solved
Specified
Staffed
Standardised
Stimulated
Streamlined

Strengthened
Studied
Supervised
Supplied
Supported
Surpassed
Surveyed
Targeted
Taught
Terminated

Tested
Tightened
Traded
Trained
Transformed
Tripled
Vitalised
Wrote

Appendix B: 50 positive adjectives

Able
Accurate
Adaptable
Analytical
Articulate
Astute
Consistent
Creative
Decisive
Dedicated
Diligent
Diplomatic
Dynamic
Effective
Efficient
Energetic
Enthusiastic

Experienced
Fast
Flexible
Gregarious
Imaginative
Innovative
Inventive
Methodical
Motivated
Organised
Outgoing
Outstanding
Patient
Perceptive
Persistent
Positive
Practical

Productive
Proficient
Punctual
Quick
Rational
Reliable
Resourceful
Responsible
Self-motivated
Self-reliant
Shrewd
Strong
Successful
Tactful
Talented
Versatile

Index

Also from JAMES INNES

Founder of The CV Centre, the UK's leading CV consultancy

So, your CV has got you an interview. Congratulations, you're halfway there.

Now, how do you ensure you get the job?

You need to know what the recruiter wants to see and hear... you need to tick their boxes.

The Interview Book is the definitive manual for interview preparation. It contains practical techniques that will put you head and shoulders above the competition.

9780273721758

9780273724636

Your cover letter is the first thing a recruiter will see.

It can make all the difference between success and failure so you need to get it right.

Brilliant Cover Letters is packed with invaluable advice that is tried, tested and proven on a daily basis.

Includes:
• Online templates available for free download and immediate use • Suitable templates for all purposes, from graduates to executives • Specific templates for jobs such as legal, medical, IT, teaching • and much more ...